O's

Little Guide to Starting Over

Other Titles in O's Little Books Series

O's Little Book of Happiness

O's Little Guide to Finding Your True Purpose

O's Little Book of Love & Friendship

O's

Little Guide to
Starting Over

The Editors of *O, The Oprah Magazine*

FLATIRON
BOOKS
NEW YORK

The Library of Congress Cataloging-in-Publication Data
is available upon request.

ISBN 978-1-250-07006-7 (hardcover)
ISBN 978-1-250-07007-4 (e-book)

Our books may be purchased in bulk for promotional, educational,
or business use. Please contact your local bookseller or the Macmillan
Corporate and Premium Sales Department at 1-800-221-7945, extension
5442, or by e-mail at MacmillanSpecialMarkets@macmillan.com.

First Edition: October 2016

10 9 8 7 6 5 4 3 2 1

When one road ends, it's time to look ahead in a new direction. And know that as far as your eye can see, the universe can see even farther.

—OPRAH WINFREY

Contents

Letting Go

The need for change bulldozed a road
down the center of my mind.

—MAYA ANGELOU

A Good Spring Cleaning

Amy Bloom

—❦—

My mother was not the traditional spring cleaning sort; she hated housework of every kind, and if I had ever seen her beat a rug or clean a window, I would have known the end of the world was upon us. But every spring she'd look at her wardrobe and mine, and eventually my children's, and declare it was time to "start fresh!" Everything that was a mistake (puce, velour, edged with rickrack) went to charity. Everything that was too large or too small went to a bigger or smaller cousin. She was smart enough to keep things that were merely, and only temporarily, out of style, and her Ferragamo pumps have now served three generations. She also made allowances for the once-in-a-lifetime (which is why I have a perfect Lilly Daché hatbox from the fifties).

I have taken her approach to heart in the matter of my closets. And I have taken her approach to heart in matters of the heart, and even of the mind.

There are things, as she used to say, up with which one should not put, and spring cleaning is a good way to deal with them. Rude children, indifferent spouses, bad bosses, lousy friends, social injustice—all have no more place in our lives than painful shoes and shirts with huge yellow stains. I'm not suggesting you throw out your children or your spouse or that you turn your entire life over to righting wrongs, but there is something to be said for addressing your burdens.

The key to addressing them is to learn to love what you have, change what you can't love, and get the hell away from what does you harm. From my point of view—that of a person with a poochy tummy—that means live with your poochy tummy (Spanx, people; it's there for a reason) but not with your toxic mother or energy-sucking job.

A good psychic spring cleaning calls for a walk through every room in the psychic house. Mark some things "Fix now," some "Try again next spring"; on some just scrawl

"Oh, well" and move on. In my real house, last spring, I threw out every spice that was more than three years old and every cosmetic that was more than two. However, the suitcases with broken zippers (and Cabbage Patch dolls and crib mobiles) remain. In my psychic house, I got rid of all obligatory social engagements that don't include family. I'm adding physical therapy on my postsurgery knee to the daily routine; I've called the nice lady who took care of my parents in their last days, as I have been meaning to do since October. And floating through the psychic rooms, I see my mother blithely ignoring dusty windowsills in favor of fresh flowers, championing repose with a good book rather than baking from scratch, and celebrating spring with a bag of things for Goodwill and a glass of Champagne.

The Heavies

Paige Williams

—❧—

The garbage bag bulges with sweaters, dresses, tunics, shoes, and belts that have languished in my closets for years, waiting for a comeback that's just never gonna come. Shirts that no longer button. Bras built for my nineties-era bust. A rain hat that has lived a life of captivity inside a drawer, never having felt a single drop.

Two Hefties sit with their mouths open, waiting to be fed. My possessions avert their gaze, as if afraid to attract attention. You there! You ugly, itchy, horizontally striped alpaca poncho bought at that street fair—to the Hefty! Random candlestick: Hefty! Mystery cell phone charger, stop trying to hide behind the Flip camera!

This lack of mercy isn't like me, and that's the point.

No matter how redundant or useless my possessions, no matter the money they cost me each time I move, an over-whelming glut of stuff has always found sanctuary in my home. But now that my home is a Boston apartment barely big enough for one human and her little dog, I've had it. I shouldn't have to spend so much time jostling for space. My energies should go to friends and family and work, not to the continual repuzzling of junk: the never-worn suits, the nearly identical pairs of boots, the proliferation of sofa pillows, the—not even kidding—velvet and taffeta ball gown, price tags intact. Barnacles, all.

I knew I had to act when I caught myself saving that rectangle of cardboard that comes at the bottom of the Chinese-takeout delivery bag because I might need it someday. So last fall I started loading boxes and bags with orphaned earrings, burdensome purses, heavy ruby curtains I haven't used since that time I had the Peeping Tom. Getting rid of such things is easy—they mean nothing to me. Even I can admit the logic of saying good-bye to all but one of three colanders, all but one of four coffeemakers. I know I don't really need a whole forest of brooms.

Steadily, the boxes and bags have filled. The surplus stuff has gone out into the world via Freecycle and eBay and the Salvation Army. There's just one problem. When I began, I figured the more I purged, the lighter and less messy my life would feel. Surprisingly, though, nothing feels less messy except the cabinets and floors.

In the past twelve years, I've lived in Charlotte, Boston, Atlanta (twice), Manhattan, Portland (the one in Oregon), Oxford (the one in Mississippi, and my hometown), Tupelo (also in Mississippi), Europe, and on Long Island.

My Oxford move, the one that signaled the beginning of the end of my four-year marriage, occurred in the wake of my father's death: I left my husband in Charlotte to teach at Ole Miss for a year and be near my family. But when the visiting professorship ended, instead of moving to the home my husband and I had just bought in Atlanta, where he had taken a new job, I ran off to Spain. After Spain, Atlanta, just long enough for the divorce. Then New York, for graduate school. Then Atlanta again, for a magazine job. Then Portland, for another magazine job. Then Tupelo, when that job fell through. And finally to Boston.

I can trace all my moves by the artifacts that came with me. The little Moroccan jar is where I stored my wedding ring when I lived in Spain. The photo of my ex and me smiling on a downtown sidewalk was taken in Charlotte before I left. The green-and-gold tin on the bookshelf contains the ashes of my cat, Harry.

Poor Harry. When I left the marriage, he—like the furniture, the Christmas ornaments, my favorite rice cooker—stayed behind. But when my ex remarried, the new wife was allergic, and Harry had to go. I was living in a two-hundred-square-foot Manhattan studio apartment with a terrier, so Harry went to stay with my mother. By the time I moved back to Atlanta and was able to reclaim him, he was skinny, elderly, mewling. The morning he could no longer stand, I took him to the veterinarian and sobbed as they administered the final injection.

Since then, each time I've passed his ashes I've thought not of his formerly happy life (sunbeams, cuddles) but rather of his miserable exile. So I take the ashes to our once-shared bungalow in Charlotte, now the home of another nice family. With their permission, I stand beneath the Japanese maple my ex and I planted in memory of my father.

"You were a good and beautiful boy, Harry, and I'm grateful that I knew you," I say. Then I open the plastic bag and pour out his remains and, to my surprise, the act feels freeing and important. For so long I believed I'd suffer horrible guilt if I ever scattered those ashes, but what I feel is closer to redemption. I've found Harry's fitting end.

And it occurs to me: What if I could find similarly soothing finales for other troubling possessions—other relics I haven't been able to part with even though they weigh me down?

There's the painting I bought after reluctantly leaving New York, where my dream life was supposed to start, for Atlanta. I hoped the painting would cheer me up, but it had the opposite effect—it seemed to get uglier and more mocking by the day. There are the books my friends have published, which only remind me that I've yet to publish my own. There's the Japanese postcard from my ex-mother-in-law, whom I loved and admired and who recently died. And there's that tiny photo in the Victorian frame.

Because it's so tiny—a mere one inch by two—I start with the photo: a shot of my old friend Carol and me. She and her husband and brother had come to visit me in Spain, and we were on a ferry to Morocco. In the background, sea and sunset. We are tanned and smiling, our hair blowing in the wind.

Carol was one of the first people I met when I moved to North Carolina, weeks out of college, to become a reporter. She was crazy-smart, funny, ambitious, a vocabulary ninja. An investigative reporter, she could dethrone a nefarious public official by 6:00 P.M. and shop for cute earrings on her way home. She set the standard for friendship, journalism, and womanhood. But somewhere amid all my moves and our respective marriages and my divorce and her motherhood and our exhausting careers, our signal friendship faded.

I could wrap the photo in tissue and store it away, or remove it from the frame and slip it into an album, but then it hits me—what *should* you do with a picture that reminds you of failure? Turn it into a portrait of resurrected friendship. If Carol meant so much to me, I should call her.

Which is exactly what I do. I leave a message; a few days later, she leaves one back. Hearing the voice triggers no pain, no guilt—just a sense of instant familiarity. It's only a couple of voice mails—we're not suddenly BFFs again—but for the first time in years, that photo doesn't feel like baggage.

In the days that follow, object after object finds its rightful resolution. The ugly painting: to eBay, and someone who will appreciate it. The books authored by friends: to their own special shelf, not as taunts but as inspiration. The Japanese postcard: properly framed, in tribute to a woman whose encouragement helped channel the course of my life.

But then I get to the rocks.

There are four of them: a mama rock the size of a flattened grade-A jumbo egg, and triplets big enough to skip across the surface of a lake. They are Italian, these rocks, dark gray with bold white stripes. They come from a secret beach in the Cinque Terre, from my last real vacation with my husband.

I wasn't able to take the lemon tree that stood outside our hotel room door, or the moon so full and bright on the water it woke us up at night. The rocks, though, I could tuck into my backpack and take home on the plane.

I have carried them with me ever since. In New York I kept them on the built-in bookshelf near the window overlooking a Dickensian roofscape of puffing stovepipes. In Portland they sat on my antique desk. In Boston, in this current apartment, so old and sloping I've shimmed every piece of furniture, they've lived in a carefully crafted pile on a bookshelf with Orwell and Melville and Auster.

I love the rocks because they remind me of Italy, and because they are beautiful and real and some force of nature made them that way. Yet every time I see them, I feel the ghost of happier times, and of my failed marriage. In fact, the marriage has haunted most of the objects weighing me down: Harry was our cat. Carol never would have visited me in Spain had I not run away from home. Though I told myself I bought the ugly painting because I was sad about leaving New York, it's no coincidence that I bought it hours after seeing my ex, his new wife, and their new baby, standing outside our formerly favorite café, in the neighborhood where they still lived in our ex-house, with our ex-furniture, and my ex-dog.

On the loneliest days I have imagined myself living there still. Us, together, and a life with all of marriage's attendant rituals and comforts.

Eight years after that breakup, people continue to ask

why the marriage ended. Among the possible answers: We were the right fit at the wrong moment. We were the wrong fit. We didn't try hard enough. Fate. All I know is that at the time, leaving felt like the only thing to do. I've lived with the yoke of that decision and its collateral damage: relatives who never had the chance to say good-bye, close friends who mourned our breakup as if one of us had died; Harry, an apparently intractable sense of loss.

Meanwhile, my ex has moved on. A few years ago, he and his wife sold the last of my things at a yard sale (after kindly asking permission), and voilà, I was gone.

I had told myself that getting rid of sentimental objects amounted to a sort of denial, and that it was braver to face old sorrows than to put them out of sight. Now I wonder if it's braver to let the wounds finally close. In giving up the rocks, I would be doing more than letting go of painful memories; I would be denying them the power to stand in the way of future happiness.

Last summer my Massachusetts friends Pam and Charlie let part of their backyard grow into a wild and gorgeous meadow. Native flowers sprang up alongside butterfly bushes and tall silky grasses. Pam and Charlie and their eight-year-old son, George, love being able to see the meadow from their flagstone terrace and from the broad windows of their beautiful house.

I no longer have the marriage, the home, the life I once lived. But I have *this* life, in which I love my work, my family, my friends, my city—and in which, thanks to this purge, I'm starting to like my prospects for getting on with things.

And so right around the time the wild meadow begins to bloom, I'll bundle up the Italian rocks and toss them into the overgrown loveliness, beneath swirling thermals that carry red-tailed hawks, in the company of two good people raising one good boy. The rocks will return to nature, where they belong, and I'll be that much lighter, readier to reach for whatever comes next.

Think Again

Maile Meloy

—⚘—

Once, during corpse pose at the end of a yoga class, I was lying on my back with my eyes closed, jiggling one foot, when the teacher came over and whispered, "Whatever you're thinking about, I promise it will be better if you can stop thinking about it for five minutes."

I knew that was true, but then I spent five minutes thinking about *why* it was true: why ceasing to think might be useful, and why I struggle with it, and whether I really wanted to be more corpselike. I do not have a quiet mind.

It's a lucky break that I'm a writer: I'm paid to turn things over and over. The artist I feel most kinship with is the French painter Pierre Bonnard, who revised his work endlessly and once had a friend distract a guard in the

Musée du Luxembourg so he could fix a painting after it had been hung.

But self-editing becomes a habit. I lose sleep rerunning conversations in my mind, knowing that all the dumb things I said (the inane questions, the indiscretions, the inadvertent slights) could have been avoided if I'd been able to take some time to consider and revise.

I also think about the tiny chance occurrences that determine the course of a life. I tagged along on someone else's blind date, as the guest of a guest of a guest, and met the man I love. I took a beginning fiction class, and a fellow student became, years later, my wonderful editor. I stood in the shade against a building and then walked away, and a ton of bricks fell and buried the spot where I'd been standing. Those accidents of fate make me think that every step we take should be weighed and measured. A different party, a different class, a longer pause on the street could change everything. How do you know which is the right path when there's no moral difference and you can't see the other options or outcome? How do you not second-guess everything?

I've been told that giving your brain a break makes everything easier. The solution seems to be in the physical, in getting out of the mind and into the body. So I've tried to find activities that don't *let* me think.

My latest attempt is flying trapeze. In theory, it's the perfect Zen practice because it happens so fast. If you're not in the moment, you'll do everything a moment too late. But I am perfectly capable of stewing and indecision in midair. When doing a trick with a full twist, I have twisted one way and then changed my mind and twisted back the other, which doesn't work—you go tumbling crazily to the net. A coach once shouted from the ground, as I reached for the bar to begin, "I can see you thinking! Stop that!"

Sometimes, magically, I *can* stop, especially when I've done a trick so often that my body knows what happens next without any meddling from upstairs. I am airborne, weightless, not thinking at all. It has a sluicing effect on the mental clutter. It's not only exhilarating, it's a profound relief.

Back on the ground, everything in my deliberating brain is a little quieter. Thinking is necessary and useful again, but there's a clearer space for it. Once in a while you need to put thoughts on hold, by whatever means possible, and just leap.

The Choice Is Yours

Martha Beck

—⊹❧⊹—

From Plato to *Star Trek*'s Mr. Spock, countless wise men have advised us to make rational decisions. Put aside emotion! Compare the costs and benefits of your options! Pick whatever option yields the highest value for the least cost! But if this oh-so-logical advice is really the way to go, then why are the Captain Kirks of the world always boldly going where passion takes them, making decisions based not on reason but on courage, loyalty, love?

As it turns out, there are good reasons logical Mr. Spock ranked second in command, while the more emotional Kirk was captain.

People who trust their gut over their brain often forge ahead with little information—risky, but at least they get somewhere. Folks with no faith in either their intellect or their instincts generally follow the path of least resistance; again, not an optimal strategy, but not paralyzing, either. Great strategists trust both intellect and instinct; they gather information until they feel they can make a good decision. But people who try to decide with the mind alone, who place no faith in their heart's desires, are doomed to stall and fuss, compare and contrast, forever insisting that just a little more information will make the choice clear. It won't.

A yogi friend of mine once told me, "The body truth goes ahead of the mind lie." When we dither over a decision, our intellect tries to gain the upper hand, shouting, *You'd better be sure! Keep your options open! Have you considered the legal implications?* and so on. Fortunately, our bodies patiently persist in telling the truth. All we have to do is listen.

Check in with yourself: Does your life feel meaningful and on-purpose at this moment? If the answer is yes, your energy is invested in living your best life. But to the extent that you feel misery, your energy is asking to be reinvested. *Misery* literally means "the feeling of being a miser." If you're miserable, stop hoarding your life energy.

Spend it now! Make a choice, any choice. If you're still miserable, you can choose again. Eventually, you'll see that all misery is simply life asking you to trade your current course of action—or inaction—for something purposeful and true.

"Are you in earnest?" says my dog-eared copy of *Faust*. "Seize this very minute. What you can do, or dream you can do, begin it. Boldness has genius, power, and magic in it." This doesn't mean you'll never misstep. It means that when you trade indecision for choice, you'll be rewarded with either success or education.

So feed your mind, but feel your heart. Trust in your truth. It will be the best investment you'll ever make.

Lost and Found

I decided to start anew, to strip away
what I had been taught.

—Georgia O'Keeffe

Coming to My Senses

Molly Birnbaum

—❀—

I don't remember the car slamming into my body, torquing my knee, breaking my pelvis, or cracking my skull during that drizzly August morning jog. I don't remember being brought to the hospital or, later, returning home. In fact, I don't remember much of the following weeks. There is one moment, however, that I'll never forget: when my stepmother held a fresh-baked apple crisp under my nose and I realized I had lost my sense of smell.

Before the accident, I had been working in the kitchen of an award-winning bistro in Cambridge, Massachusetts. A recent college grad, I had cast aside my degree in art history to pursue my dream of being a chef. I washed dishes, peeled garlic, and watched and learned from my more experienced coworkers as they moved gracefully around the tiny kitchen. Arriving home in the early hours of the morning, my clothes saturated with the scent of fry oil and butter, I felt perpetually exhausted. But I was happy.

After I left the hospital, I couldn't return to the kitchen. I learned that when I fractured my skull, my olfactory neurons, which lead from the nose to the brain, had been damaged. I was thankful to be alive, thankful that I would recover from my other injuries. But I was devastated when doctors told me I would probably never regain my ability to smell.

The flavor of food is reduced to a mere whisper when its scent is lost. I still had my taste buds, which register salty, sweet, bitter, and sour. I could sense temperature and texture. But nothing more. The nuance that makes a bite of steak, spoonful of ice cream, or sip of coffee delicious had vanished. I began dousing every morsel I put in my mouth with Tabasco sauce just to feel the spicy kick on my tongue. *How will I cook?* I wondered. It looked like the end of the life I aspired to, the one that revolved around the stove.

But I'm stubborn. I refused to leave the kitchen behind. I loved the culture of food, the joy of bringing people together around a table, so I decided to teach myself how to cook by relying on my other senses.

I began with sound. I listened—carefully, closely, my ear hovering above the sauté pan—as a pat of butter melted over medium heat. I concentrated on the subtle sound of its liquefaction, focusing on its chattering foam, and waited for the moment it grew suddenly quiet—which meant that it was ready for me to slide a pink-cheeked pork chop into the pan. I paid attention to the sizzle of salmon under the broiler and the crackling sound of sautéing mushrooms releasing their juices, adjusting the heat if the noise grew too loud or too soft. The melodies of the kitchen came together in a song I'd never heard before.

I came to prize my sense of touch. Using my fingertip, I'd gently press a rib-eye steak on the grill and compare its flesh with the palm of my clenched fist to figure out when the meat was ready to come off the fire, perfectly rare. I kneaded bread dough with greater care, my fingers intuiting when it was elastic and smooth enough to create a light, airy loaf. My hands had never felt so alive.

I looked at the plate with newly artistic vision. I realized that arranging red and yellow roasted beets on a bed of bright green arugula or scattering bloodred pomegranate seeds on a tawny ochre chicken tagine could stimulate the appetite in a different way than scent. I learned to inhale with my eyes.

Finally, I embraced my newfound reliance on temperature and texture. I even baked my own apple crisp, luxuriating in the silky, soft fruit beneath the crumbly crust, the icy rivulets of vanilla ice cream melting on top. I reveled in the soft innards of a warm baguette and the cold creaminess of fresh goat cheese, the crisp-tender bite of asparagus poached just so.

It was only when my sense of smell began unexpectedly to return that I truly understood the connection between smell and taste. The first scent I noticed was rosemary, dark green and woodsy. Soon after came the earthiness of chocolate, and then the watery aroma of cucumbers, which was surprisingly strong. When I could finally smell the rich, ripe edge to blue cheese that enhances its pungent sour taste, the pleasure was so intense I stood up from the table. Today, nearly seven years later, I can smell almost everything again. I'm lucky, I know. This awareness follows me around like a benevolent spirit, reminding me to pay attention and enjoy every meal, bite by miraculous bite.

The Voyage Out

Sarah Broom

—⁂—

Up until my time in Burundi at Radio Publique Africaine, I was best at setting myself apart, as a monument of sorts, so that no one could enter and look around. I did this not only with those I loved romantically but, perhaps more important, with family and childhood friends.

Friends like Alvin Jarvis, whom I grew up with and who died at the age of twenty-two in a car accident. The last time I saw Alvin I was back home in New Orleans for a summer break from college in Texas. Alvin broke away from his hard-looking friends and walked over to me and grabbed at me for an embrace, but my grasp remained loose. I did not hold tight onto his back, the way he held mine, but rather beat it a few times as if it were a drum. He asked me how school was. I said, "Fine," looking down at my toes. Alvin had never left New Orleans and I had, and I let that be the chasm. I understood without *understanding* that by avoiding Alvin, I hid from myself.

But in Burundi, looking down or away never worked. I had arrived in that tiny Central African country unmoored, without a familiar language or geography, and let loose from my personal mythologies. At work at the radio station, I was forced to rely on my Burundian coworkers for more than I had ever needed from anyone. And that forced an internal movement. Whenever I tried to look down or around or away from someone, they became more curious than before.

A few other things happened, too: I met a man whom I recognized but didn't yet know, and in time he helped show me to myself. Sometimes a person can do that. He loved me, and I felt thoroughly and keenly myself in his presence. He—and Burundi and its people—showed me a kind of caring that taught me the value of looking straight at things.

One day I was stranded on the side of a mountain road on my way upcountry, waiting while my flat tire was being fixed. It was broad daylight, and surrounding me were young boy soldiers wearing fatigues and carrying sawed-off shotguns with the barrels wrapped in tape. At first I was full of fear, and with good reason, but then I noticed the slow way the men were surrounding my car as I waited hour upon hour and life moved along—women carrying babies on their backs and plastic containers of palm oil on their heads. And suddenly someone had sugarcane and was offering me some. No words spoken, but the sucking and spitting out of sugarcane while the radio played a Phil Collins song. In that moment I learned something of brotherhood and trust and the human condition. All of us together like that.

And later, a gloomy Sunday when I was sitting in my African house, the solitude burning, with no place to go and no one to talk to. With the banana trees shimmying outside the window and the sound of rain beating down the roof drowning my thoughts, I opened up a novel and out of it fell a Polaroid of Alvin, my childhood friend. I was surprised and set off-center.

James Baldwin once wrote: "To encounter oneself is to encounter the other: and this is love." It took me a long time to know what he was talking about, but Alvin's picture that day forced me to think about the enormous costs of pushing him away, and that felt like a waste of good love. I took the picture and sat it right where I could see it. It is now, always, right where I can see it.

I know this: It is possible to stumble upon oneself in the process of looking onto and receiving others. I had perhaps come into the world alone, but it was populated with other people when I arrived. People who might love me, see me, teach me things. And so I glimpsed, somehow, in Burundi, the nature of connection, which is to say, the nature of love. And there cannot be, I have come to know, one without the other. Simple sounding, yes, but not actually, and I have traveled quite a long way to understand that.

Beyond My Imagination

Suzanne McMinn

—❧—

Eight years ago, I was a novelist living in a comfortable suburban home. I had financial security and a husband. But my happily-ever-after wasn't turning out happily, and so I moved with my three children to a century-old farmhouse in West Virginia. I was ready to be challenged by the unknown.

Boy, was I challenged.

I'd always dreamed of having a farm, but I soon realized I didn't know the difference between hay and straw. I'd never been close to a chicken, much less a cow. (A cow that would kick me, and the milk bucket, repeatedly.) There were many low points in the months to come, as I battled the woodstove that I couldn't light and chased my goats when they jumped the fences. But I was also living a life beyond my imagination, and no hardship was bigger than the satisfaction of finding the courage to live it. As a writer, I know change is part of the plot; that's how your character evolves. With change, there is grief for what has been lost, but also opportunity—and the choice of how to see it.

Choose wonderful.

Just One Good Thing

Junot Díaz

—◈—

It wasn't that I couldn't write. I wrote every day. I actually worked really hard at writing. At my desk by 7:00 A.M., would work a full eight and more. Scribbled at the dinner table, in bed, on the toilet, on the No. 6 train, at Shea Stadium. I did everything I could. But none of it worked. My novel, which I had started with such hope shortly after publishing my first book of stories, wouldn't budge past the 75-page mark. Nothing I wrote past page 75 made any kind of sense. Nothing. Which would have been fine if the first 75 pages hadn't been pretty damn cool. But they were cool, showed a lot of promise. Would also have been fine if I could have just jumped to something else. But I couldn't. All the other novels I tried sucked worse than the stalled one, and even more disturbing, I seemed to have lost the ability to write short stories. It was like I had somehow slipped into a No-Writing Twilight Zone and I couldn't find an exit. Like I'd been chained to the sinking ship of those 75 pages and there was no key and no patching the hole in the hull.

Want to talk about stubborn? I kept at it for five straight years. Five damn years. Every day failing for five years? I'm a pretty hard-hearted character, but those five years of failure did a number on my psyche. They just about wiped me out. By the end of that fifth year, perhaps in an attempt to save myself, to escape my despair, I started becoming convinced that I had written all I had to write, that I was a minor league Ralph Ellison, a Pop Warner Edward Rivera, that maybe it was time, for the sake of my mental health, for me to move on to another profession, and if the inspiration struck again some time in the future . . . well, great. But I knew I couldn't go on much more the way I was going. I just couldn't. I was living with my fiancée at the time (over now, another terrible story) and was so depressed and self-loathing I could barely function. I finally broached the topic with her of, maybe, you know, doing something else. My fiancée was so desperate to see me happy (and perhaps more than a little convinced by my fear that maybe the thread had run out on my talent) that she told me to make a list of what else I could do besides writing.

I'm not a list person like she was, but I made one. It took a month to write down three things. (I really don't have many other skills.) I stared at that list for about another month. Waiting, hoping, praying for the book, for my writing, for my talent to catch fire. A last-second reprieve. But: Nada. So I put the manuscript away. All the hundreds of failed pages, boxed and hidden in a closet. I think I cried as I did it. Five years of my life and the dream that I had of myself, all down the tubes because I couldn't pull off something other people seemed to pull off with relative ease: a novel. By then I wasn't even interested in a Great American Novel. I would have been elated with the eminently forgettable New Jersey novel.

I stopped going to bookstores and reading the Sunday book section of *The Times* and hanging out with writer friends. The bouts of rage and despair, the fights with my fiancée ended. I slipped into my new morose half-life. Started preparing for my next stage, back to school in September. (I won't even tell you what I was thinking of doing, too embarrassing.) While I waited for September to come around, I spent long hours in my writing room, sprawled on the floor, with the list on my chest, waiting for the promise of those words to leak through the paper into me.

Maybe I would have gone through with it. Hard to know. But if the world is what it is, so are our hearts. One night in August, unable to sleep, sickened that I was giving up, and even more frightened by the thought of having to return to the writing, I dug out the manuscript. I figured if I could find one good thing in the pages, I would go back to it. Just one good thing. Like flipping a coin, I'd let the pages decide. Spent the whole night reading everything I had written, and guess what? It was still terrible. In fact, with the new distance, the lameness was even worse than I'd thought. That's when I should have put everything in the box. When I should have turned my back and trudged into my new life. I didn't have the heart to go on. But I guess I did. While my fiancée slept, I separated the 75 pages that were worthy from the mountain of loss, sat at my desk, and despite every part of me shrieking no no no no, I jumped back down the rabbit hole again. There were no sudden miracles. It took two more years of heartbreak, of being utterly, dismayingly lost before the novel I had dreamed about for all those years finally started revealing itself. And another three years after that before I could look up from my desk and say the word I'd wanted to say for more than a decade: Done.

That's my tale in a nutshell. Not the tale of how I came to write my novel but rather of how I became a writer. Because, in truth, I didn't become a writer the first time I put pen to paper or when I finished my first book (easy) or my second one (hard). In my view a writer is a writer not because she writes well and easily, because she has amazing talent, because everything she does is golden. In my view a writer is a writer because even when there is no hope, even when nothing you do shows any sign of promise, you keep writing anyway. Wasn't until that night when I was faced with all those lousy pages that I realized, really realized, what it was exactly that I am.

The Woman Who Fell to Earth

Martha Beck

I spent at least half my childhood drawing. By the time I got to college and signed up for my first drawing class, I was pretty comfortable with a pencil. My teacher was a brilliant draftsman named Will Reimann. To impress him, I fired up all my best tricks: lots of varied lines, fade-outs, soft gradients. One day while I was drawing, something landed on my sketch pad. It was a mechanical drafting pen.

"Use that from now on," said Mr. Reimann. And he smiled the smile of a man who has hatched an evil plot.

How I hated that pen! It drew a stark black line of unvarying thickness, making all my faboo pencil techniques impossible. You'd think my teacher would've been helpful, or at least forgiving. But no. He'd glance at my awkward ink drawings, groan, "Oh, God," and walk away holding his head in his hands, like a migraine sufferer. My art grade plummeted. I writhed with frustration.

A few weeks later, though, as I sat in another class taking notes with the pen of doom, something happened. Without my intention, my hand started dancing with that horrible pen. Together, they began making odd marks: hatches, overlapping circles, patches of stippling.

The next drawing I completed won a juried art show. "How did you figure out a drafting pen could do this?" one of the judges asked me.

"I failed," I said. "Over and over again."

Since then I've had many occasions to celebrate failure, in myself and in others. And I've noticed that the primary difference between successful people and unsuccessful people is that the successful people fail more. If you see failure as a monster stalking you, or one that has already ruined your life, take another look. That monster can become a benevolent teacher, opening your mind to successes you cannot now imagine.

My dog-groomer friend, Laura, breeds and shows prize-winning poodles. One afternoon she arrived at the dog park looking thoroughly dejected.

"What's wrong?" I asked as our pets gamboled about.

"Ewok," said Laura, nodding mournfully at her well-coiffed dog. "He didn't even place at yesterday's show. Didn't even place! And he hates to lose!" Her voice was so bitter I winced. "He should have been best in show," she said. "Look at him—he's perfect!"

I looked at Ewok. He looked fine—but perfect? To me, saying a poodle with long legs is better than one with short legs seems absurd. A poodle's a poodle, for heaven's sake. I think Ewok would've agreed. He certainly didn't seem to be the one who hated losing. He'd discovered a broken Frisbee and appeared to be experiencing the sort of rapture Saint Teresa felt when visited by God.

Laura's desolation stemmed not from what actually happened at the dog show but from her ideas about failure. Lacking such concepts, Ewok was simply enjoying life. Going to dog shows and winning, going to dog shows and losing, going to the park and scavenging—from Ewok's perspective, it was all good. Meanwhile, Laura's thoughts about losing had tainted these experiences. Thankfully, she'd managed to avoid the pitfall worse than failure: success.

I can't count the number of times people have told me,

"I hate the job I'm doing, but I'm good at it. To do what I want, I'd have to start at zero and I might fail." Dwelling on failure can make us miserable, but dwelling on success can turn us into galley slaves, bound to our wretched benches solely by the thought, "I hate this, but at least I do it well." This is especially ironic because researchers report that satisfaction thrives on challenge. Think about it: A computer game you can always win is boring; one you can win only sometimes, and with considerable effort, is fun.

With time-killing games, where the stakes are very low, pretty much everyone's willing to risk failure. But when it comes to things we think really matter, like creating a career or raising children, we bear down, tighten up, and absolutely refuse to fail. Anyway, that's the theory. The reality is, we are bound to fail. By refusing to accept this, we only make things worse. Conversely, if we own our failure openly, publicly, with genuine regret but absolutely no shame, we reap a harvest of forgiveness, trust, respect, and connection—the things we thought we'd get by succeeding.

I owe much of my ability to accept failure to my son, Adam. Though I bred young, never smoked or drank, ate right, and all that, Adam showed up with an extra chromosome. Oops. From the word "go," I'd failed to make him a successful student, athlete, rocket scientist. In my mind, nothing could compensate for such massive failures.

Adam helped me discover that the bigger the perceived problem, the better it delivers failure's great gift: freedom from attachment to ideas about success. A lucky person escapes her enemies. But a really lucky person (as the poet Rumi puts it) "slips into a house to escape enemies, and opens the door to the other world."

This can happen in tiny ways and huge ones. The day my pencil-proficient mind accepted failure and allowed my hand to start dancing with that mechanical pen, a door opened on a new way of drawing. Accepting that I'd failed to create a "normal" life for my child blasted away much bigger assumptions, bone-deep beliefs like "Successful mothers have smart children" and "My kids should never fail."

This hurt like a sonofabitch, but when the rubble cleared, I found myself in a world where all judgments of success and failure are arbitrary and insignificant, as ridiculous (no offense) as the American Kennel Club's definition of the "perfect" poodle. Without judgments, it's obvious that joy is available in every moment.

And so failure did for me what it's done for so many

others: softened, mellowed, calmed, enriched, and embold-
ened me. The poet Antonio Machado expressed it this
way:

> *Last night as I was sleeping*
> *I dreamt—marvelous error!—*
> *that I had a beehive*
> *here inside my heart.*
> *And the golden bees*
> *were making white combs*
> *and sweet honey*
> *from my old failures.*

I can't say I look forward to the failures that await me.
But they'll be along in no time, so I feel lucky to know what
to do when each one arrives. My strategy will work for you,
too. Unscrunch. Exhale. Let go of "Oh, no!" and embrace
"Oh, well . . ." Then, whatever door opens, walk through.

Take Two Risks and
Call Me in the Morning

Bonnie Friedman

One ordinary September day, walking down my street to
Key Food in Brooklyn, I saw the shape of my life. It was a
narrowing corridor. I had just turned forty-five, and although I still felt like a girl in pedal pushers with every
possibility ahead of me, it occurred to me that humid
morning that the years were flipping by.

Before I reached the corner, I realized that I might
never see China or the Red Sea or the outback of Austra-
lia. I recalled being a college junior, lying on my back in a
sunny field in Spain, surrounded by other students, and
assuming that I would someday visit almost every place on
earth—as if my life were a Spanish galleon that would carry
me about. It never occurred to me that I'd have to pay my

fare, say good-byes, or even choose my direction. I simply thought of the future as an endless opening of possibility, like gates flung wide.

Now I recognized that my existence had become quite confined. I was following the same routines every single week—going to the same places with the same people, eating the same familiar foods—and I was afraid of change. Over the years, I had discovered that travel, while fabulous, made me feel glutted on sensation: I'd find myself longing for my rickety desk and my home in the city where I grew up. I didn't really want a footloose life.

But I did want *more* life. So I decided to take two risks a week. They could be tiny or not, it didn't matter. The thing was to consciously open up, to expand the range of what I'd get to experience. Not to choose my adored but predictable chicken and cashews at the Chinese restaurant. Not to maintain the same safe but isolating formality in the writing seminar I taught. Two risks a week seemed manageable, and I started right away. I brought the intimidating students I taught—a smart, urbane, and disdainfully reticent group—a strange tropical fruit called mamey. One of the students had mentioned this fruit in a piece about Cuba, saying its taste was indescribable.

I held one up for everyone to see. "Class," I said, "today we are going to describe the indescribable." Then I cut into the fruit and distributed the slices. At first the students' almost haughty demeanor seemed to reflect the vibe, "Is this really worth my time?" But after we sniffed, chewed, and scribbled together, they grew less cerebral and more expressive; the room grew noisy with laughter and discussion.

A few days later, I poked my head into an imposing colleague's doorway and invited him out for coffee. I tried to quell the horrible feeling in my stomach as he gazed at me. But soon I heard myself blurting: "I'm trying to take two risks a week. This is one."

"I'm not so scary," he intoned. We had our coffee two weeks later. Miraculously, he became my one friend in the department—and I his. He told me that in the five years he'd taught at that school, nobody other than the department head had reached out until I appeared at his door.

After an amateur Gilbert and Sullivan performance on New Year's Eve, I approached one of the singers as he walked up the street. I did it only because it was already Wednesday—early Thursday morning, really!—and a new year beginning, and I hadn't yet taken a risk that week.

"Thank you so much," I told him. "You were the best. I just kept waiting for you to come back onstage."

He looked startled. "You're kidding!" he said. "Wow!"

As he walked away, I felt a moment's awe. He hadn't known how good he was.

Since then I've fed a baby rhinoceros, eaten ceviche, phoned my councilman's office, and tried a new Laundromat, all by telling myself that it didn't matter what the outcome was; my goal was simply to take this risk. It became almost fun to sit down with the phone book, my heart pounding as I dialed *The New York Times* to ask to be connected to the City desk—and not hang up when someone answered with a gruff "Hello?" Then to feel the champagne-y joy of getting the name of an editor to whom I could submit a story. I hadn't been treated dismissively, as I'd feared. All the energy that had gone into anxiety and restraint became celebratory instead.

Almost every single risk ended happily. It's true that *The Times* didn't accept the piece I sent, and the ceviche puckered my mouth, but I now know that I love papaya salad, and kumquats, and the jewel-red meat of beets, and I've worked past midnight in the copy department of a fashion magazine, and I've agreed to teach essay writing to a group of women theologians in San Jose. I'd be scared (some of the theologians are quite eminent), except they are my risk, and so I'm simply looking forward to meeting them and finding out how they'll broaden my life.

Taking two risks a week has had the result I craved that morning almost a year ago. It's allowed me to live in an ampler world. It's let me be someone else—someone gutsier—in small doses, and then savor the rewards. And when the councilman helped me, when the baby rhino chomped the apple chunk, when the performer's face lit up—what amazement swept over me. This is my China, my outback—my own beloved familiar world opened up to allow in the light.

A New Day

If trying to find a way when you don't even know
you can get there isn't a small miracle,
then I don't know what is.

—RACHEL JOYCE

The Truth Is in There

Caitlin Flanagan

—⚜—

In the summer of 2008, I was diagnosed with a metastatic recurrence of the breast cancer I thought I'd seen the last of five years earlier, when it had been a relatively laughable stage III. (In case you're not familiar with cancer staging, I'll quote Emma Thompson in *Wit:* "There is no stage V.") I heard the doctor say "liver," I heard the doctor say "lung," and both words sounded so much like death that for a while I couldn't hear anything else. When I went for chemo, I didn't bring photographs of my two young sons the way I had the first time through. I couldn't bear to look at their faces as I was failing them. It was a summer of darkness and dread.

And then one day, for no discernible reason, it occurred

to me that instead of continuing to sit in bed bald and weepy, maybe I should try to cheer up. It was such a crazy idea, I decided to go with it. Being at that moment of limited resources—a TV remote, a laptop, and a can of Ensure— what I did was patch myself through to Oprah.com.

I came across three videos of Oprah interviewing a sixty-something woman with short white hair, extraordinary violet eyes, a mesmerizingly calm and benevolent manner, and the strange name Byron Katie. At the age of forty-three, Katie, as she is called, had had a life-changing realization about the importance of living in the reality of the present moment. All the suffering that goes on inside our minds, she told Oprah, is not reality. It's just a story we torture ourselves with.

The last thing a cancer patient with tumors in her liver wants to hear is that her suffering exists only in her mind. But Katie had something else to offer, too, or so she said: a simple, completely replicable system for getting rid of the thoughts that make us suffer. "All war belongs on paper," she told Oprah, and then she explained how to go to battle: You write down each and every stressful thought, and then ask yourself four questions about it.

Is it true?

Can I absolutely know it's true?

How do I react when I believe this thought?

Who would I be without the thought?

Afterward, when you have completely wrestled the thought to the ground, you replace it with a "turnaround"— an opposite thought, one that is "as true or truer" and that doesn't cause you suffering.

I grabbed my journal and got to work. Almost immediately I felt a shift; it was as though, at least for a few moments, my problems started to ease. Yes, it was true that I'd been diagnosed with stage IV cancer. On the other hand, if you pushed me—did I absolutely know I had cancer?—I had to admit I didn't. I was in the middle of chemotherapy, after all—for all I knew, it was working beautifully. The thought that I had cancer made me feel terrified and immobilized. Without that thought, I was free—I was just myself, sitting on my bed with the windows open, completely alive and enjoying the breeze.

I made pretty good progress that first day or two, asking the questions, following them up with a turnaround, and feeling better each time I did, but I had a hunch that I was going to get only so far on my own. There was something eating away at me that I couldn't even identify, let alone question. And this is when things got a little bit crazy, because after seeing how much I'd changed my mood by simply writing some questions and answers, it seemed that the next thing to do—the only thing to do— was sit down and talk with Byron Katie herself.

Byron Kathleen Reid grew up in and around Barstow, California, in the barren high desert 100 miles northeast of Los Angeles. Her father was a railroad engineer, her family moved back and forth between Barstow and neighboring Needles, and her childhood was unremarkable. When Katie—a pretty, intellectually uncurious California girl with a pile of tawny hair—arrived in Flagstaff to attend Northern Arizona University in 1960, she was not in possession of a burning desire to make her academic mark.

She fell in love, dropped out before the end of freshman year, and married her boyfriend. They had three children, but the union faltered, and they divorced. Three years later, Katie bounced into another bad marriage. Once again stuck in Barstow, she began to sink into a pit of addictions, anger, overeating, and misery that led her to near constant thoughts of suicide. She was, seemingly permanently, in hell.

In 1986, out of options for what to do with herself, Katie got her husband to drive her to a halfway house in Los Angeles, where the other residents were so terrified of her rages and sulks that they refused to share a bedroom with her, insisting she sleep alone in the attic.

Her self-esteem so low that she didn't believe she deserved to sleep in a bed, she chose instead to bunk on the floor, and it was there—hunkered down in an attic, seething with loneliness and confusion—that Katie went to sleep one night, hours away from what would be her awakening.

If you've ever had the experience of waking up in an unfamiliar room, when, for a few disorienting seconds, you can't for the life of you place where or even who you are, then you know what happened to Katie the next morning—with one exception. For her, the sense of "I" didn't immediately click back into place. The data didn't upload. Maybe it was a neurological event, maybe it was enlightenment, but one thing is certain: The burden of her self-identity was lifted.

A cockroach crawled across her foot that morning in the halfway house, and she woke up—or, as she says, somewhat confusingly—"it" woke up. Not "it" as in the cockroach; "it" as in the pure consciousness inside her own head. Katie had the sensation of seeing the world through perfectly neutral eyes, with none of her own backstory attached.

"There was just awareness, no story. It"—that pure, unencumbered consciousness—"had never seen anything before. It had never been born before." (It was the kind of revelation that's usually accompanied by the munchies.) "I realized," she says, "that the mind projects the whole world."

What she means: There is reality, and then there is the movie your mind projects about that reality. There is the dress, and there is the movie that tells you how you look in the dress. Your mind *projects* the movie that tells you that you're about to be fired or that you've ruined a friendship or that you have no sense of style.

That morning in the attic of the halfway house, Katie realized that we all have full permission to walk over to the movie projector and yank the plug from the wall. "There are two ways to live your life," she says. "One is stressed-out, the other is not. One hurts, one doesn't. Either way, you're living it. Look, if you're having a nightmare, don't you want to wake up? That's what I'm inviting people to do—wake up to reality."

People in Barstow noticed the transformation as soon as Katie came home. Everyone wanted to know what she'd done to become so suddenly joyful, so able to live in the moment and embrace life. Whatever it was, they wanted some, too. So Katie started talking about the four questions she asked herself when she had a problem—and in those conversations were the seeds of what would eventually become an empire. She began inviting people to spend time with her so they could observe her way of life; soon, small groups of students were gathering in her home. After she was invited to speak to a gathering of psychologists in the Berkeley area, the small groups turned into growing crowds of followers at seminars devoted to what came to be known as The Work of Byron Katie—the deceptively simple and wildly successful method of dealing with life's emotional pain that is based on her four little questions.

In service to The Work, which by now has been embraced by millions, Katie runs a 28-day residential program called Turnaround House (catering to addicts and anyone with "deep-seated self-defeating behaviors"), and does endless pro bono sessions, in particular at prisons.

Although she charges a fee for personal consultations, her Web site includes all the materials needed to do The Work free of charge. It also features videos that show her guiding people through The Work. Sometimes these people's problems are so dire and their wishes so plaintive that her questions—though asked in the most gentle, coaxing way—can seem cruel. "Is that true?" she keeps prodding men and women who have admitted a tormenting fact about their lives. "Is that really true?" Yet, invariably, with Katie's help, these people appear to find their burdens suddenly, almost miraculously lifted.

And that is why, in the summer of 2008, being in need of a miracle of my own, I found myself driving to Byron Katie's house in the horse country of Ojai, California, about an hour and a half northwest of my home in Los Angeles. I went with a friend, and we made good time up the coast. The day had an air of inevitability, even magic. (When you're forty-six and cancer-ridden and screaming "road trip!" every ten minutes en route to seeing a guru, it's easy to get carried away.) Then we arrived at the white house situated in a vast Elysium of orchards and gardens and protected by a large wrought iron gate, and the weirdness of what I had set in motion hit me.

As I waited for Katie in the sweeping, light-filled foyer after her husband let me in (her doting third husband, Stephen Mitchell, a best-selling writer and translator), I couldn't help thinking, "So it's come to this: The drugs didn't work, and now I'm seeing some kind of faith healer." A very well-to-do faith healer with a thing for white. Not like the big white light you're supposed to see at the end, but the white everyone warns you not to buy furniture and rugs in because it will get filthy. But this wasn't filthy; it was radiant. Windows, light, beauty.

And then—there she was, coming toward me, smiling. She wore Eileen Fisher clothes the way they were made to be worn (in deference to physical reality, in celebration of older-woman sensuality). Even though we'd never met, her smile made me feel like she'd been waiting forever to see me again. "Hello, sweetheart!" she said, and hugged me. I'm not a hugger, but I went along, smiling at the floor.

I followed her down a long white hallway into a sitting room next to her bedroom, and I accepted a glass of cool water, and then I told her what was happening to me. Or rather, I read aloud from the manifesto of suffering I'd written in anticipation of this moment. I read about having cancer, and how I had two small children who needed me, and why my particular diagnosis was very bad, and how the chemo was exhausting, and how superscared I was, having no idea if the treatment was going to work, and how I hated being bald, and on and on and on.

When I finally gave her a chance to talk, I figured she was going to try to make me feel less scared about my prognosis, or convince me that even as a baldy I could feel beautiful. Instead, totally out of left field, she said, "Your children need you. Is that true?"

I looked at her like she was out of her mind. "Yes!" I said. "They're nine years old! They're little boys! They just finished fourth grade!"

To which she said, easy as pie, "Uh-huh. Your children need you—is that true?"

Now I was getting angry. I wanted to walk right out of there, but I said, "Yes, it's true! My children obviously need me"—you freaky kook lady, whose check I'm gonna cancel the second I get home.

And she said, just as calmly as if she were asking where I'd bought my sweater, "Where are they right now?"

"They're with their dad," I said. "My husband."

At which point a tiny glimmer of light came on in my head, but I was so not going to notice that glimmer because no way was I going over there. Then she said, just as placid as could be, "Is he good with the boys?"

Of course I took it hook, line, and sinker: "Oh, yeah, he is the best dad in the *world,* and he does so much with them, and the three of them have a great relationship—you cannot imagine. He should get dad of the year."

And just as matter-of-fact as ever, she said, "Your children need you. Is that true?"

I just sat there and sat there and sat there—and then *kaboom* in my mind like you cannot believe: I realized that Katie had nailed it.

It wasn't the cancer, or the chemo, or the baldness that was keeping me in hell—it was the terror of thinking that if I didn't make it, my boys wouldn't either. But they would. They would! If, in fact, I didn't make it, my boys would be okay. Their dad would take care of them. And all our relatives. And everyone at church. They'd be fine. They could and would make it without me if they had to.

"That's right, sweetheart," Katie said simply when I blurted all of this out. "How narcissistic to think they couldn't live if you didn't live."

She had found the thought I hadn't had the nerve to

look at on my own—the thought that was so huge and scary, I couldn't even see it. She'd found it not because she knew me better than I knew myself, but because she sat with me and listened. She was present. She was in the moment—which is exactly where The Work has enabled *me* to stay (enjoying my life, my husband, my boys, instead of drifting in a sea of existential dread). And if you had been sitting in the garden outside Byron Katie's open window that summer day, overhearing first my fear and then my shock and then my confusion and then my anger, you would also, finally, have heard my laughter, all thanks to the question that by now has changed my life.

"Oh, honey—is that true?"

Getting Lighter

Lauren Slater

—❧—

I remember the day my depression and I met, when I was five—bright white with summer heat, the roses burning on their bushes, the whole world suddenly flattening and colors draining from their forms, leaving behind etched outlines of things that had once been vibrant. I don't have a reason. I only know that as I grew up, so did my depression, moving around in my body, making lead of my legs, filling my head with fog. Now, as I near fifty, my depression, it seems, inhabits my heart and takes the shape of a slim speckled stone, its contours changing over time while its essence stays the same. My depression does magic. Poof! Each day it disappears at around four or four thirty in the afternoon and then—slam!—returns at dawn, sapping my energy, stealing color from trees and leaves and socks and spoons, everything still and silent as if under some spell.

I'm not complaining, or if I am I don't mean to be. Thanks to antidepressants I reliably have seven hours, more or less, of good clear time, and I strive to use it well, ticking off items on my to-do list, trying to tie up my business so that when the fog comes, at least things will be in order. Still, seven waking hours is not a lot, less than half the sixteen or so most people have. Last year I bought a large clock that I hung in the hub of our house—the kitchen—right where I can hear it best. My kids complain about the hourly clang, the audible ticks, but I've come to count on the constant reminder of my dilemma and its demands.

It should come as no surprise that much in my life falls by the wayside. My taxes, for instance, are always late. My children's doctor and dentist appointments are missed, rescheduled, missed again. I shop for their clothes flying through Target as fast as I can, ripping from the racks the pants and skirts that society demands they wear. And for many years my own wardrobe was not nearly as nice; on a typical day the best I could do was a pair of pajama pants, the elastic gone loose at the waist, and a stained gray shirt. My hair was two-tone: the bottom an anemic yellow, the roots wiry white. On the windowsill in the bathroom sat a box of dye. I kept meaning to color my hair, but I never found the time.

The truth of the matter is, I was a schlump, a frump, my clothes secondhand and without style, dirt under my fingernails, the nails themselves without shape, their excess hacked off every few months, making my stubby fingers look still more so. I'd never had a pedicure and couldn't see why I ever would, what with only seven productive hours to my day. My husband, who is himself a bit of a slob, was nevertheless somewhat sobered by my lack of grooming and tried, on occasion, to motivate me with gifts: petite bottles of perfume I never used or earrings in a box tied up with red ribbon. His offerings were shy and hesitant—at odds, he felt, with his feminist leanings but speaking to some deeper desire: to have a wife who looked, if not good, at least good enough.

For so long, I rarely had the time or energy to shower. Because of this, some months ago I developed an abscess at the base of my spine. At first I thought I'd bruised my coccyx, but as weeks went by the pain only increased, and when I reached my hand around I felt a hot hard lump weeping fluid. My physician told me I had what is called a pilonidal cyst—a bad one. The next day, I lay on my belly on a surgeon's steel table as the cyst was drained, a procedure so painful it lies beyond language. The surgeon, employing no anesthetic beyond a useless slug of Novocain, sliced into the boil and squeezed its contents so hard I heard the spurt and saw, smeared on a large white cloth, blood and pus and a shocking amount of green goo, the smell fetid and wrong. He stuffed gauze and a wick into the wound and told me to keep myself clean and come back in two weeks to have the wick removed. On the way out he handed me a prescription for OxyContin, which I immediately filled and took four of, even though the label capped the dose at two. I lay on my bed and watched the air eddy and swirl.

The cyst was caused by dirt working its way under my skin. I realized, even in my stoned state, that my self-neglect had gone past the point of acceptable. I was now getting infected. Depression or no, I'd have to start devoting some time to grooming, stepping into the shower in the morning and coming out wrapped in a soft, fluffy towel. I thought of a study I'd read a long time ago, so long ago I could no longer recall the paper or book from which it derived, but the gist of which had stayed with me: that mood is influenced by outward appearance. This had seemed odd when I'd read it and still seemed odd now, mood so deep and internal, so unrelenting and unyielding; how could clean hands and hair possibly shift that behemoth? And yet studies show a strong link between improved "ADL" skills—activities of daily living, such as showering, combing your hair—and a lessening of the symptoms of depression.

A psychologist by training and degree, I decided to construct an experiment. Was it possible that if I spruced up, my mood would follow suit? What would happen if, during my downtime, my depressed time, I made an effort to look nice?

My plan was to dress myself up every day for three weeks and see whether I could alter the inward me by changing the outward me. My resolve to follow this path increased when I saw in our town circular an ad from a woman named Dianne who called herself a beauty consultant; for a small fee she would come to your house and teach you how to put your best foot forward, covering everything from makeup to clothes to shoes to hair.

Three days later, Dianne pulled into my driveway and hauled two bulky cases from the trunk of her car. She had a black furze of curls and reddened lips and a floral tunic with a scoop neck and a big bow in the back. As she came up my walkway, her slacks fluttered in the wind.

With falling faith I opened the door and said, "What's in the bags?" and Dianne said, extending her hand, "Hi, I'm Dianne." I shook her slender paw, noting the lustrous pink of her nails. She set the cases on the floor and said, "These? These are before-and-after photos, from clients I've worked with." I sat with her in the living room, I with my weeping boil and dumpy clothes and she in a cloud of lilac scent, as we flipped through the photos and designed my personal program, Dianne standing up, stepping back, scanning me from tip to toe, and then pronouncing, after several moments of consideration, one word: *hair*.

I nodded. Hair. We would start there.

The appointment was for ten o'clock, smack in the middle of my daily despair, so when the day rolled around

I could barely drag my carcass from my sleep-warmed sheets. I heard my doorbell ring and then, "Yoo-hoo? Yoo-hooo?" accompanied by the clickety-clack of Dianne's stilettos as she came to haul me out of bed and into the stylist's chair.

The salon was all spiral staircases and dizzying racks of shampoos, conditioners, curl creams, mousses, gels, sprays. I was ushered toward a changing room, told to take off my top and replace it with a crinkling black gown that snapped shut and, for good measure, tied at the waist. The gowns were made for slender women; my bulk strained the snaps so the fabric pulled at my chest and left visible gaps I wanted to hide with my hands. But "Yoo-hooo," Dianne called, tapping on the door of the dressing room, so out I stepped, into the sweet-smelling humid air.

My stylist was Andrew. He looked about sixty years old. "He's the best here," Dianne whispered. Andrew stood behind my seat and looked at me in the mirror. He then walked around to face me, knelt, and reverentially took my cheeks between his hands, moving my head left, now right, studying me. He nodded crisply, sprang to his feet, and picked up a pair of scissors that looked preternaturally huge, like something out of a storybook, clack-clacking as he aimed them at my hair.

"Wait a minute," I said. "Wait, wait"—and so Andrew stopped in mid-motion, the huge silver scissors frozen. I said, "Aren't you going to ask me what I want?"

"You don't know what you want," Andrew said. He was correct. I had no idea. "Let me take care of this," he said. And then he went to work. He dove into me, lifting me up in layers, splicing me sideways, long wet hanks falling onto the floor as I eyed them with rising fear: Would anything be left? Snap, snap, said the scissors, dark and dripping hanks continuing to fall. Andrew circled, spun me around in my seat, pumped me up, then down, and then, suddenly, with no slowing, he stopped. My hair, which had before fallen past my shoulders, now came in close to my neck, which for the first time in years was bare to the air. Andrew circled me slowly, with great ceremony, moving me around until at last I fully faced the mirror, my hair still damp but drying now, released from the weight of its long length, all cowlicks and curves, my face in a frame of waves. "You like?" he asked, and then, without waiting for a reply, he stood behind me, leaning down so our faces were side-by-side in the mirror.

"Listen to me, Lauren," he said.

"I'm listening," I said. He was so close I could smell his cologne, a tang of pine and winter.

"Lauren," he said again. "You have heavy hair."

I nodded. Dianne, standing a little way off, nodded, too.

"All that weight," Andrew said.

I suddenly wanted to weep.

"I've released you," he said, "from all that weight, and now"—he bobbed back up like a jack-in-the-box—"and now, look what we have here," and he cupped the back of my head while tweaking a curl, pulling it past its kink and then letting it loose so it fell back into perfect position. "I'll bet you never knew how stunning you were, under all that weight."

"She is stunning, isn't she," said Dianne, smiling.

"Stunning?" I said. That was impossible. But improved— that could certainly be. *Weight weight weight,* that word *weight* kept going through my head. And then it was as if everyone disappeared. I lost the sounds of the salon, the hot hair dryers and women whispering. Now there was just me and my mirror, which I leaned into, the curls so curly, the anemic yellow chopped off, my hair ash-brown and veined with glossy whites, the look light and alive, my face indeed framed, the pink seam of a new side part making my nose and my mouth and my eyes seem somehow softer, with sparkle. I blinked. Still there. Cautiously, I touched my hair. Then I pressed my hand down, hard, to see if I could squelch the sudden spirals; they bounced back. They would not be banished. I gave Andrew a twenty-dollar tip.

At home, alone at last, I headed for the bathroom, where I turned on the shower and stood under its spray, clearing my neck and back of prickles, careful not to wet my hair. And then, instead of stepping out, I turned on the tub, shut off the spray, and before long was standing ankle-deep in wet warmth. Slowly, so slowly, I lowered my heft into the filling cavern, the water roaring as it spilled from the spigot. When had I last taken a bath? And why was I taking one now? On the way out of the salon I had purchased bath beads of every color. I poured them in. I leaned back and planted one foot firmly on the tub's tiled wall so that my leg was out of the water. Using my husband's razor, I, for the first time in years, shaved my legs, discovering as I did that, despite my weight, I still had the curve of a calf, the soft silk of an inner thigh. I stayed in that tub a long,

long time. Then I toweled off carefully and put on a dress. I felt lovely. And where was my depression now?

My husband would be home soon. I went downstairs to wait for him in the kitchen, barefoot. When he came through the door, he said, "What happened to you?" I cocked my head coquettishly and looked at him. I liked the way his eyebrows arched and his eyes went wide. I walked over to him and tilted his chin downward. I gave him a kiss, a good kiss, a real kiss, the kind of kiss a woman with a headful of curls could give. He responded in kind. This kiss went on for maybe a minute. I felt infused. I felt as if we were exchanging vitalities. When it was over we smiled at each other in the secret way that couples do. "I got my hair cut," I said. "Did you ever," he replied, and then, "Wow."

The next week Dianne took me shopping and I got my face done at a makeup counter. I bought a plum lip liner that, when I used it, announced my mouth, plus a matching lipstick that filled in the announcement and gave it some substance. I liked most of all my nut-brown eyeliner and the silver and almond eye shadows, all three colors working in concert to give me a deeper, dreamier look. By the time we left the store, I had also purchased a long gray skirt, a peasant blouse with a ruffled neckline, and espadrilles with straw wedge heels and ribbons that crisscrossed the calves. The season was changing, the damp early darkness of winter giving way to a warm spring, the rhododendrons blooming early.

At first it felt funny—no, it felt hard—to arise each morning and dress up, applying my new makeup carefully, leaning in to line my eyes and then, with the miniature wand, sweeping silver across my lids, taking the tweezers and plucking my brows into slim little arcs. While some women find this process fun, I did not. It was a discipline, forcing myself to flick through the new outfits I'd purchased and pick one for the day while my insides were dreary and dark.

But after several days of dolling up, I began to notice my reflection in my kitchen's wall-size windows, my lines leaner and flowing, my skirt so long it puddled past my ankles and swished when I walked into my study. I'd pull out my chair to start work. It felt odd to be so dressed just to write. I had no power lunches or afternoon meetings or presentations to attend; it was just me and my computer, and yet, as the days passed and I showered and put on outfit after outfit, brushed blush across my cheeks, my work started to change. Prior to dressing up I had been a plodding sort of scribe, but now words were coming to me more quickly and people were rising up out of the page and populating my stories with their authentic idiosyncrasies; these fictional characters were often accompanied by people from my past, and they, too, came up out of the blank page to meet me—because, I could only think, I was finally dressed for the occasion.

My long-lost libido returned; it was more tempered than it had been when I was in my twenties, but as my husband fumbled with the many buttons and zippers and snaps of my new clothes, these barriers to bare skin increased our arousal and pointed to yet another reason to engage in self-adornment.

Not since I was a teenager had I taken such care in how I looked. I was not able to completely dress my depression away, but when it—slam! bam!—returned each day, it had to tussle with a woman whose heels hoisted her high, who could confidently kneel and cup the faces of her children in her hands, who knew how to tend others because she tended herself. I washed my daughter's bleeding knee with the same cloth I swept each morning across my own dream-creased face, kissing her wound and leaving on it an impression of my lipsticked mouth, proof not only that I was here but that I could care.

It's too soon to know whether my newfound belief in the power of beauty will become a way of living. But I can say, for sure, that entering into beauty did not in any sense diminish me as a woman, an artist, a mother, a wife. I did not become all preen and polish, with nothing of substance to offer. I look people in the eye. I dream I am 12 feet tall.

One day a friend suggested we hike Mount Caesar, not far from where I live. Previously I would not have accepted such an invitation, worried that depression would drag my steps down, but before I could even consider that as a possibility I found myself saying yes. Yes. So we went. And we made it. Huffing and puffing and streaming with sweat, we made it to the top. The wind blew. There was an old rusty trash can and a peeling picnic table and ground gone gold with pine needles. There was a rocky escarpment we crawled out on to look down into a lake so pure and blue it seemed to possess some sort of living intelligence, a huge eye of water beaming back at us.

"Swim?" my friend said.

It was a warm day, the temperature well into the eighties. My friend, who is thin, stripped off her clothes and, suddenly, even though I was fat, I followed suit, because I had some chutzpah now. That's what it came down to. Chutzpah. Dressing up gave me the confidence to dress down, to strip. My friend dove first and I dove second, feeling my body arc out over the escarpment and sluice through the summery air and enter the water as fast and fierce as a spear driven downward, everything gone green, and then finning fast upward and breaking the surface with a gasp and a shout: "Oh, my God!" We laughed and laughed.

And then we treaded water silently and swam around. I could see the top of the mountain from where I was and also a field of wildflowers, lilacs, and lupines in every imaginable color and great white wheels of daisies amid emerald spikes of grass, and it occurred to me that beauty is not outside nature; it is nature, the way the world is meant to be.

As the sun started to set we climbed onto the shore and clambered back up the rocks, our clothes in sun-warmed heaps; we dressed ourselves and started back down the trail. Even though we were sopping wet we didn't shiver, our shirts and shorts still soaked in sunlight, the chocolate bar I'd stored in one of my pockets completely melted now so when I thrust my hand in, searching for the necklace I'd removed before I dove, I felt a thick warm gush and, laughing, lifted my smeared fingers and licked, savoring the flavor, grateful I could taste this good.

From Shock to Awe

Kelly Corrigan

—❦—

Shortly before I turned thirty-seven and my older daughter turned three, I was diagnosed with stage III breast cancer. A year later—chemo, surgery, and radiation behind me—I was ready to return to my former life. Little did I know that recovery also has its stages. The main difference? On the other side of treatment, bigger numbers are better.

Stage I: Increased Surveillance

My marathoner friend was in Boston when the bombs went off, and for several months afterward, whenever he lit his janky gas grill, the resulting pop made him jump. Cancer is like that. For a while, ordinary things feel dangerous. That scar tissue/headache/out-of-the-blue lower back pain could be evidence of recurrence, right? Should you call your oncology nurse? Schedule a visit to the mammography center? (Recurrence anxiety loves a doctor's appointment.) But then you start to wonder where diligence ends and paranoia begins. And after one too many panicky speed dials, you start to fear it's the latter—which is why this stage also involves pretending you're no longer living from scan to exam to blood draw. The rest of the world, especially the rest of the world who loves you, wants you to stop being shocked by sudden noises. They want you to let it be over, come back to life, even celebrate, whether you're ready or not.

Stage II: The Slip-Slide

How is your heart? Your bone density? Your recall? During active treatment, I would have traded every one of them for a clear mammogram. (For all I knew, I had.) Slowly, though, I stepped from the bottom rung of the ladder, where survival is everything, to a more demanding place, where I wanted bones that would take me the distance, not to mention my old hair and eyelashes. In other words, I began to hope for more from life than life itself. I wanted to be comfortable and attractive. And come to think of it, I wanted my Irish luck back. I realized I'd entered a new stage the day I got my first post-treatment parking ticket. "Un-be-f*cking-lievable!" I scream-whispered, my daughters trailing behind me, arguing over who had to walk the dog when we got home. "Give me a break!" Just a month earlier, my two girls had been everything and enough. If only I could see them graduate, marry, become moms themselves, that's all I could ever ask for. And then . . . there I was, asking for a bit more. Could I see them safely into their adulthoods, and could they not bicker, and could we not get a $65 ticket for underfeeding the meter by three minutes? Could I have those things, too? This, I realized, made me no better than my girls, who begged for a dog, who loved the dog with such passion for the first, oh, twenty-four hours, but for whom, soon enough, the dog became not so exciting. My survival, which had once been cause for Dom Pérignon, was now not quite enough of "a break."

Stage III: Connection

There is nothing wrong with using a tennis ball to play tennis. But you can also toss one into the dryer to fluff your comforter. Likewise, you can use toothpaste to soothe a bug bite and Coke to rub out rust. It's similar with cancer: Whereas initially I had applied my experience in the obvious way—to connect to fellow breast cancer patients—I soon started swapping stories with all kinds of cancer survivors, then with friends with other diseases (Crohn's, depression, shingles), then with people whose ailments weren't even physical. A bout of breast cancer, it turns out, has uses as varied as a Q-tip—because the broad-stroke pattern of crisis is so consistent. There is shock, followed by resolve, then digging for answers, then work—so much work—until, eventually, acclimation, both physical and emotional.

Within that pattern, naturally, there are switchbacks and stalls, like the desire to dissociate from the community you've been thrust into. I almost threw up the first time I set foot inside the University of California, San Francisco's Comprehensive Care Center and joined the stream of thin, slow-moving, low-voiced, gray-skinned people. I didn't want to be one of the pitied, the struck-down. But remembering that resistance came in handy when talking with my friend Joan, who didn't want to be one of the housewives whose high-flying husbands cheated, or my friend Bill, who didn't want to be one of the financial services guys who got laid off, or my neighbor Tara, who didn't want to be one of the parents who put their kid on Ritalin. I understood completely. (There's a reason people trust people who have been tested. We know things.) Cancer is a growth hormone for empathy, and empathy makes us useful to each other in ways we were not, could not have been, before.

Stage IV: Wide-Angle Amazement

It's one thing to long for life in the operating room or infusion chair. It's another to feel, in the middle of our nothing-special, could-be-better, hanging-in-there existence, how deeply we ache to be here. In the final stage of recovery, we have a shot at achieving the most elusive and divine of emotional states: awe. This is where we privately, humbly approach the well-known facts of existence—we are tiny, we have laughably little control, it will end—and sit with the staggering truth beyond: Small and fleeting, yes, but we are here. We are here.

The Teardown

Paige Williams

—❦—

The teacher wants me to make a Japanese ham sandwich: I'm to stand with my face to my shins and chest to my thighs in perfect vertical union. That is, I *am* the sandwich.

I would say I look more like a jelly roll. My flabby abdomen won't let my forehead anywhere near my knees, and my legs tremble as I try contorting myself into a position my body neither recognizes nor endorses.

The students around me are tanned and toned and very nearly nude. Every body glistens. We're in a Bikram yoga studio, after all, where the heat is set to 105 degrees and the humidity to 40 percent, to facilitate flexibility. The men wear nothing but shorts; the women rock hot pants and halters. Because I'd rather lick the sweat-soaked carpet than bare my wretched flesh, I have on the hot-yoga equivalent of a snowsuit: calf-length sweatpants, a jog bra, and a T-shirt. I'm huffing harder than a serial killer. And we're only on posture number one.

Posture number one of class one of day one. Assuming I survive, I'll make the ham sandwich and about two dozen other postures every single day for the next two months, for the notorious sixty-day Bikram challenge. I'm subjecting myself to "Bikram's torture chamber," as founder Bikram Choudhury himself calls this regimen, because the program promises renewal from the inside out.

I need to change so many things about my life it's hard to know where to start. I need physical, spiritual, mental, muscular, molecular transformation. I need to stop treating my body like a landfill. I need stability. I need a reset button. I'm divorced, in debt, and eighty pounds overweight. I don't sleep. I have no love life. Wellbutrin and Lexapro, in their little amber bottles, rattle around my life like maracas. My career? Mr. Toad's Wild Ride. One minute I'm winning the magazine industry's top writing honor, the next I'm taking an editor job. Then losing that job. Then living back home with my mother in Mississippi.

"Do this yoga for sixty days and it will change your body, your mind, and your life," says Choudhury, a former Indian yoga champion. And indeed, some believe that his heat-centric sequence of yoga postures is a transformative agent, easing the symptoms of depression, diabetes, carpal tunnel syndrome, fibromyalgia, migraines, arthritis, back pain, and heart disease, all while relaxing the mind and slimming the body.

"Can't you just do all that by, like, *running* for sixty days?" a friend asks. Good question, but the answer doesn't interest me. None of my past fitness activities—racquet sports, cycling, jogging, gym circuit training, kickboxing— seem catalytic enough for the depth of change I'm after.

Is it possible to pinpoint the moment a life swings out of balance? For me it happened, to borrow from Hemingway, "gradually and then suddenly."

The slope started getting slippery when my father died. My marriage failed a few years later. I stockpiled debt by following divorce with grad school (expensive) in New York (superexpensive) and by self-medicating depression with stuff.

Then my body began throwing me curves. Fibroid tumors in my uterus, disappearing eggs and estrogen that made chaos of my hormones. I worked incessantly to get out of debt; thus, I was "too busy" to care about wellness. Raised an athlete, I exercised less often than Thomas Pynchon appeared in public. A pattern set in: anxiety, work, self-isolation, medication, sobbing mixed with flurries of rage.

You know what helps such situations? Pie. Also Big Macs. Nighttime triggered a food free-for-all. Because I ate poorly and didn't exercise, I slept badly. Because I slept badly, I woke up harried with no time for breakfast. I'd have coffee for lunch, looking forward to all the junk I'd eat later that night.

For a while, my career was going well. In the fall of 2008, I assumed the editorship of a small magazine out West. For a bajillion reasons, it didn't work out. I'd say the center couldn't hold, but I'm not sure there ever was a center. Wherever my slide started, it ended here: Stress + sugar + carbohydrate overload − exercise + insomnia − adequate water + self-loathing − romantic intimacy + regret = meltdown. One particularly fraught Friday morning I failed, completely, to hold my tongue with the magazine's publisher. By Monday morning, I was in the unemployment office.

For three months, I had a headache. My whole body ached. My hair fell out. Most nights, I went to bed with a heated terry-cloth beanbag around my neck like a boa. If I slept, I'd grind my teeth. (It was an old problem: Years ago, when I was married, my then-husband woke me one night and said: "Are you eating *candy*?")

While looking for a new job, I had time to start exercising again, to eat right, drink water. But I didn't. It was easier to retreat to the land of dim rooms, dark chocolate, and all-day television, to outfit myself entirely in caftans.

And then one afternoon, while lying fully clothed in my childhood bed on a beautiful and utterly wasted Mississippi summer day, it suddenly occurred to me: I wasn't dealing with a debilitating condition or an abusive husband or unremitting poverty or the death of a child. I'd done this *to myself*.

I realized it was either get up—I mean really get up—or die. I don't know why, but I thought of Bikram yoga. I had tried it a few times. I remembered appreciating most of all the permission to be quiet. I recalled the yoga room as a place where I could finally breathe.

Now, as I start the sixty-day challenge, I need to know the depth of the damage. I decide to undergo a physical.

In the days before my workup, I did one last gastro-nostalgic round of Burger King, Wendy's, and Taco Bell. If there'd been a Dairy Queen within twenty-five miles, I'd have hit that, too. I'm eating Papa John's breadsticks even as I call to *make the appointment*. I don't even like bread-sticks.

Good nutrition doesn't come naturally to me. In my home state of Mississippi, the fattest state in the nation, a vegetable isn't considered edible unless you've cooked it in bacon grease. That history shows in my stats. Before check-ing me for heart disease (clear) and cancer (also clear), the nurse weighs me in at 208 pounds—83 pounds more than I'd like to weigh (I'm 5′ 5″). "Your physical exam," the doctor's detailed report will say, "reveals ... evidence of obesity."

Obesity?

Federal guidelines say you are clinically obese and therefore in danger of liver and heart disease, diabetes, sleep problems, osteoarthritis, and cancer if your body mass index (BMI) is 30 or higher. Mine is 34.6. For a woman my age, overall body fat should be between 23 and 33.9 percent; mine is 42.1. I am basically a gel.

I am also very close to being prediabetic, and my LDL

cholesterol, the bad kind, is high enough that most doctors would prescribe medication to treat it. I'm told that I need to improve my diet immediately and exercise at least thirty minutes a day—for the rest of my life. Breathing and stretching are, the doctor says, particularly beneficial. Both, as it happens, are central to Bikram yoga.

Bikram Yoga Memphis, the studio closest to my mother's home in Tupelo, Mississippi, is cruelly located a few doors down from Muddy's Bake Shop, which some consider the best cupcake pusher in the city. For the first seven of the sixty days, my goal is twofold: Stay out of Muddy's and do not throw up in class.

On day one, the instructor stands up front, on a carpeted podium. The goal for beginners, she says, is just to stay in the room, to learn to breathe. "Feet together, heels and toes touching, let's begin," she says. In a Bikram studio, only the teacher speaks, delivering Choudhury's almost incantatory instructions. Class takes place in a large, rectangular studio with thin carpeting and a floor-to-ceiling mirror on one long wall. The lights—*so bright*. You're supposed to be able to see yourself, meeting your own eyes as you move through the postures to develop a relationship with your mirrored self and start being kind to her.

Day after day I blunder through twenty-six postures and two breathing exercises, including physical impersonations of a rabbit, a camel, a human bridge, a flower petal blooming, an eagle, a cobra, a corpse, a triangle, and a pearl necklace. My body simply won't bend. My breath is so loud, it attracts attention. Even lying in savasana—flat on my back with my arms by my side—feels strenuous, because my heels won't touch and the junk in my trunk puts a pinching arch in my back. Obviously, this is going to be more complicated than some sweating and some stretching, and—voilà!—solace and skinny jeans.

But it's not only the extra weight that interferes. My brain never shuts up: *My bra's too tight. My ponytail's too high. This carpet stinks. Is that cellulite on my biceps? I'm thirsty. Maybe it'll rain today. Why does everybody in here have a tattoo? Do I need a tattoo? I might be having a heart attack. I'm exhausted—I'm done with this posture. I'm gonna bake me some chicken tonight.*

One day as we perform the standing series—the first 50 minutes of class, where the heart rate rises—I become suddenly certain that I'm going to projectile-vomit my lunch onto the woman in front of me. I attempt to flee the room.

"Sit back down! Sit back down!" the teacher says.

"You'd rather I throw up on the carpet?" I say.

"You're not going to throw up," he says. "Lie down. Just breathe."

This panicked feeling is what they call the "yoga truck." When the yoga truck hits, all you want to do is get out, or lie in savasana and count ceiling tiles. After fifteen days, I am sore and discouraged and sick of being wringing wet, and I feel utterly overwhelmed by everything I'm supposed to remember, sometimes all of it at once: Lock your knees, contract your abdominal muscles, chin down, chest up, focus only on yourself in the mirror, quiet your breath, pulling is the object of stretching, if you're falling out of the posture you're not kicking hard enough, chin up, eyes open, let it go, just be here, have compassion for yourself, kick harder—kick, kick, kick, kick, kick, kick, kick!

Flat on my back, I silently rant at myself. *I hate you. I hate this class. I hate this stupid stomach and these enormous boobs. I hate Ben & Jerry and KFC and the Lay's potato chip company. My car smells like a yoga studio, and for what? After nearly three weeks, my clothes aren't any looser. I may as well go on a cupcake crime spree for all the good this is doing.* My classroom emotions have started to veer like mountain switchbacks: confidence panic euphoria despair.

"How long did it take to get yourself into this mess?" a teacher asks one day.

"Years," I say.

"Well, then," he says, "it'll take awhile to fix."

"Elbow hurt? Arms hurt? Back hurt? Hair hurt? Hands hurt? Good for you," Choudhury sometimes says to students during particularly challenging moments in class. "All the pain in the world is not going to take happiness and peace away from you. If anybody can make you angry, you are the loser. If anyone can steal your happiness, peace, away from you, you are the loser."

You'd have to be in the studio to understand the power of words like these. The teachers' instructions and insights become like a mantra. As I lie in savasana, half dead with exhaustion, just listening to the instructors talk about strength and determination—about the integrity of the *attempt*—propels me through the remaining postures. I may not do the moves perfectly or even well, but by week four I'm doing them. I've stayed in the room, which calls upon reserves of calm I didn't even know I had. Instead of thinking, "I can't do this," an alternative occurs to me: "I *am* doing this."

The first demon to go is the stiffness. The second is the headaches. As I reach the halfway mark of thirty days, I feel more relaxed. I stand straighter. I can touch my toes. People tell me my skin looks great, my eyes brighter. One day in the parking lot, a woman driving a Mercedes cuts me off, and instead of fuming, I simply let it go—lady wants to be a jerk, let her be a jerk; it's got nothing to do with me.

I'm drinking water now—not enough, but more than before. I've changed my diet to lean meats and vegetables and have set myself back only once, with a pair of chewy Chips Ahoy cookies (120 calories) one particularly rough night alone. The food changes don't feel like sacrifice. In fact, I was hungrier on the drive-through diet of probably 3,000 calories a day than I am now on half that amount.

On day 30 I take a few measurements. My weight has dropped to 198—a long way from my personal goal of 125, but I'll take it. Wii Fit tells me my BMI has fallen from 34.6 to 32.7. I've lost 2.5 inches in my hips, 2.5 in my bust, and one inch in the all-important waistline. Also, I got a job—a terrific one. Another city, another magazine. I'll start work after I finish the Bikram challenge (assuming I finish the Bikram challenge).

At one point, Choudhury himself swings through Memphis to promote his newest book. I talk with him before the crowded book signing, a conversation that encompasses the fifth dimension, Jupiter, and a parable about a wooden bird.

"What's the most important thing in your life?" he asks me.

"Is it bad that I can't answer that question?" I say.

"I ask the same question around the globe," he says. "They answer God, water, wind, family, children, love—all bull. The most important thing in your life is you."

By day 60, I hope to understand what he means.

Five weeks in, I'm working on committing, which is hard for an inveterate leaver. I've left cities and jobs and dear friends and good men. I've been in such a hurry to flee some situations and get on to the next that I've left clothes in the closet, food in the fridge. In Bikram class, I've already tried to leave once, but that didn't work. So knowing that I can't leave, I quietly protest my captivity by pretending.

The yogis call this the games stage. I'll do anything to buy myself a break. One day, I could do triangle posture if I wanted to, but I don't want to, so I breathe dramatically and pretend to be near collapse. (Result: I kind of really *do* feel near collapse.) The teachers recognize the tricks because they've tried them all themselves. If I say I don't feel well, they shake their heads and say, "Do yoga like a champion." If I admit (or claim) that I'm exhausted, they say, "No mercy." I've heard an urban myth about an instructor in California who was in the middle of teaching a class when a rat showed up in the back of the room. "Rat! Rat!" the students yelled, and the teacher said, "That's not a rat. That's the manifestation of your fears."

One afternoon in the middle of ustrasana, or camel pose—a backbend that some consider the toughest posture in the whole practice—it occurs to me that if I can remain calm and focused while in such a physically stressful state, I can get through anything.

At the beginning of the challenge, a 60-day goal felt daunting. Around day 20, it felt impossible. Around day 50, I started getting that giddy, generous feeling that comes when the bad date (or vacation or visit) is almost over and you can sense freedom. Only I don't want freedom.

On day 60, as the final class ends, I would like to say the clouds part and the angels weep. When the teacher utters his final words and we as a class take our last measured breath, I expect a rush of emotion, but what I feel is calm, and satisfied, and like I now have a refuge, a resource—a blueprint.

I'm so eager to see what the diagnostics show, I hardly even notice the needle sucking blood out of my arm. My last Bikram class ended just an hour ago and I'm already back at the doctor's office for my final physical.

Here's what I already know: The 60-day challenge got me out of bed and out of my own head and showed me the futility of self-flagellation and regret. I've stopped taking the Wellbutrin and Lexapro, and my depression, while still with me, feels manageable. I must not be grinding my teeth anymore, because I no longer wake up with a headache. Now I'm ready to see what Bikram has done for my body.

Weight: I've lost 14 pounds.

Waist: 5 inches, gone.

LDL cholesterol: 108.

BMI: 32.3—down 7 percent.

"Everything changed," says the doctor. "And in the right direction."

I've found a great yoga studio in my new city. I recognize none of the other students, of course, but everything about the postures is now familiar. I do not, and will never, love every class. Some days I'd rather stroll through Times Square in a string bikini than spend another ninety minutes in that steam box. Yet the best of Bikram redeems those days. The best of Bikram is like being in love. It's like taking in that first breath of springtime air, seeing green tips on the stems of dogwoods.

One Saturday during those sixty days in Memphis, I'd walked out of class and into a golden morning. Everything I saw seemed urgent and worthy and beautiful. I passed two old men hauling four small horses. I saw a field of yellow wildflowers. At a traffic light I pulled up behind a LOVE WINS bumper sticker. At the grocery, as I wheeled my empty cart back to the corral, an old man said, "Baby, let me push that over there for you. It'll be my good turn for the day." When I got in the car, Lloyd Cole was singing— I'm not kidding—that song about Eva Marie Saint in *On the Waterfront: "All you need is love is all you need."* The whole grueling 60-day experience was worth that one euphoric morning. Because I'd forgotten I could even feel that way.

Like Myself

Katie Arnold-Ratliff

—❧—

Once, when I was eight, my mother took me to work with her for the day. She passed a hopeful note across her desk: *Do you want to be like me when you grow up?*

Some days she stayed in bed with a box fan trained on her face, the white noise a roar. Some days she baked for hours, the kitchen's prisoner. Some days she asked me to lie with her in the waterbed she shared with my father, where she held my hand and said again and again, "You're my best friend." Her need was thick and humid, a weight on the atmosphere of my life.

A word could wound or please, enrage or disappoint. Once, when I was nine, she crumpled when I whined that she'd eaten the last waffle, believing I'd called her fat.

Once, when I was six, singing in the back of our weary old minivan, she turned from the passenger seat and bellowed, "Enough," her glare so murderous I couldn't meet it. When I glanced back, her blue, relentless eyes were still fixed on me, laden with disgust.

I practiced invisibility. Once, I limped around with a broken ankle for an afternoon until someone noticed. I resolved to stop speaking. I vowed to do better, to *be* better. If I got an A, she was unmoved; had I done my best? If I did my best and got a B, she was unmoved; one must rise to every challenge. What I remember of my mother from those years is what she wanted from me, which was love and excellence; and what I could give her, which was too little of both.

The year I turned twelve, I broke. At night, every night, I'd lie in my bedroom overlooking our quiet street and sob for hours, watching headlights project tree limbs against the wall. The pain took the form of a voice. *You're poison. You deserve nothing good. People who say they love you are lying.* I took it at its word. I didn't tell my parents.

Before long, the voice plagued me day and night. *You shouldn't exist. Do what's right. Rid the world of the burden of you.* When I was seventeen, I started ditching class.

My grades circled the drain. I'd go to punk shows to get kicked in the teeth. I'd go to work at a coffee shop before school, and after, to not be home. I told only my boyfriend that my mother was imploding. She went online for hours, chatting up phantoms; she barked at my little sister and brother, at my father, at me, if we got close to the screen; she wore headphones in the car to mute our bothersome voices. She no longer slept. She went to the gym daily, for hours. For months she didn't know where I applied to college. It didn't occur to me to tell her.

I was a thousand miles away, at a summer camp for young writers, when she e-mailed: *You're a great kid, I'll miss you.* I was relieved, for a moment, to feel the heft of her hatred lift. And then I understood. I ran, hard, to a pay phone. I still don't know what she did or didn't do. No one told me, and I didn't ask. I just know that when I returned a month later, she was our ward. We watched her shower, waited outside the outpatient facility while people in her group described driving off cliffs, gassing themselves in their kitchens. We learned words and phrases: *psychotic break, bipolar disorder, lithium.*

I started college, developed a stomach stitch so gutting I couldn't fully stand for nine months. I saw a doctor in week three of month eight, around the time I quit school. Class required stillness; stillness was intolerable. I drove my tires bald, spent rent money on clothes, gained thirty pounds, drank like I was being paid to. I had friends, none of whom knew. I crawled back to school, eked by with a C average. I married the boyfriend.

The autumn I was twenty-nine, I found a book on adult children of mothers like my mother, parents like my parent. I shook as I read: "You squelch your anger and your sadness and your fear." "You . . . find it difficult to accept caretaking when it's offered." "You learned early in life that your needs wouldn't be met." "You fear that while you *appear* responsible and loving, if you really let someone get close, they'll discover the bad you." I shook and shook and I read, and *still* didn't see what I was, what I needed.

The February I was thirty-two, the sky shed snow in days-long salvos. I got the job done at work, got the dishes done at home, got high daily. I rarely slept. I went to therapy to discuss my failing marriage. I didn't tell my doctor the voice's allegations: *You're a net loss, you're a sort of criminal, your life is a series of monstrous delinquencies.* I didn't tell her I routinely dug my fingernails into my palms hard enough to leave bloody crescents.

Therapy clichés exist for a reason, which is to say that most roads led to childhood. My wise doctor was a Greek chorus: "I feel like I'm parenting my husband," I said. *Like you parented her!* "I can't count on people." *Like you couldn't count on her!* "Right, okay," I said, shredding tissues and thinking about *That.*

I thought about *That* in images, sensations: the knotted belt, the doorknob. Life, narrowed to a pinhole, then gone. I thought about *That* when friends asked, "How are you" and I chirped, "Pretty good, you?" I thought about *That* when I wrote, paid bills, watched movies—when I did things the living do. Then one night I counted it off: weepy at twelve, stony at seventeen, bereft at twenty-four, desperate at twenty-nine. Now this. The voice hissed, *It'll only continue.* What choice was left? A rule all writers learn: The right ending is the one that feels inevitable.

The belt, hung from the doorknob, buckled beneath the chin; the forward pitch; the blood-filled eyes, antic pulse; the thorax close to cracking. Seconds became hours. The sounds were inhuman. *What a shame*, I thought, fading. *What a waste.* Then, unbidden: My sister's velvet cheek. My brother's wiry hands. My doctor sitting opposite my empty chair. The dear friend, the proxy mother, who loved me, taught me, telling her child what I'd done. And my husband, and my husband, and my husband.

I rose, and, when I could breathe, said aloud, "You are very sick." The relief of those words! The rightness, after all had been so wrong. The deservedness of a designation—*sick*—on which my mother had no monopoly. I confessed what I'd done, what I'd nearly done, to my doctor. She said, "We're not dicking around anymore."

Then, the journey back: the proper pills, double sessions, a second doctor to complement the first. The voice grew faint, a mutter from another room. Not long ago, my mother turned to me at a stoplight and said, weeping, "I'm sorry for the way I was." She takes her medication. I take mine. We go to our therapists. We go on.

My marriage ended, the vows grown obsolete; a different person had made them. But I've promised other things. That I will let others care for me. That I will save the only life I can. That I won't die before I've learned to live.

That day at her office, Mom asked if I wanted to be like her. I jotted down my answer, then passed the note back. *No*, I wrote. *I want to be like myself.*

Matters of the Heart

We come to know ourselves in a different way
when we fall in love, and whatever happens to that
relationship, we are changed.

—ETHEL PERSON

Cups of Men

Heather Sellers

One hundred cups of coffee with one hundred men.

I got the idea from a lawyer friend, who married a handsome furniture maker in Maine who owned more books than she did. "Sometimes," she said, "I met three a day. You only need fifteen minutes." It took her two months. She quickly lost count.

After six months, I am at four.

We meet in a coffee shop parking lot. He springs out of his enormous red convertible, more like a boat than a car, and thrusts into my hands a fat library book. He looks ten years older than his photo and roughened, like someone has taken the smooth young version he posted and rubbed sandpaper over it. I stare at the book he's handed me, turn it over. It is a book of ideas and complaint. He is ranging around the parking lot on foot—big loops. Why is he ranging around the parking lot? Why am I holding a fat library book? "Finally," he says, rovering up to me, beaming. "Finally someone in this godforsaken place gets me." I kneel down, set the book on the pavement, pretend to tie my shoe.

I tell the next man about the coffees. He wants to know what number he is. "I want the T-shirt," he says. "Number X, with the cup, you know. That's what I want." He pats his front. He says he wants to be ninety-nine. He, too, has books, paperbacks in his backpack. Two backpacks. One is his office.

I feel so bad for them all. The man with a part in a play who could talk of nothing but the play. The play is his life. Both will start soon. The man in white kneesocks and black sneakers who chose a coffee shop across from the mental institution. It was very distracting. The whole time he talked, I kept trying not to think he'd come from across the street on a pass.

The chef/Hemingway aficionado/sea captain (age fifty-three, two kids at home, blue eyes) who said he would be divorced but the economy was really bad and he couldn't do that to his wife. She had a boyfriend. He was excited about dating.

It's like going to the pound and I am a nice dog from some other pound.

I felt afraid one time. He yelled, stood, holding his coffee aloft in the Buzzatorium. "I'm not a loser! I'm not a loser! I do not think I'm a loser!"

I feel forensic. I feel I should be getting paid, because this feels hard, like a job, all these coffees. And I have to get specifically dressed for it and leave my house.

They behave as though they're on job interviews or in sales positions, leaning forward, pitching. Maybe it's the caffeine, but the men *do not shut up*. Not nervous-talky, like a girl gets, but sales-talky, rushed, forceful, boasty. They have a few prepared questions, but they aren't wanting the information. They're checking off boxes. *Asks questions*. I'm talkative, and I can't get a word in edgewise. They talk for thirty minutes and I wonder how my friend kept it to fifteen. She lives in New York. In the Midwest, everything is slower. I listen too much. I need exit strategies. I need less hope. In the Midwest, we're shadowed by hope, enveloped by it.

Part of me wants them to keep talking; it's similar to reading a mediocre novel. I know I'll never finish, but I can't quite put it down. I know it won't get better. Can it get worse?

When I stand up to say good-bye, the men say, "Wow. You are a great conversationalist."

My friends are married people and stunned. "Why are you doing this?" "I could never do it." We say this same thing about tragedy, as though we have a choice. About wheelchairs and cancer and missing limbs. Looking for love isn't a tragedy or a defect. It's a situation.

I'm doing this because I've been divorced three years and I haven't had a single date. No one has asked me out. I called the single father on my street before Christmas and asked him to go out for a drink. He said he didn't have any money right now.

My friends think I am trying too hard. "Stop trying and then it will happen!" "When you give up, that is when it will happen." They think I am so happy alone and I will not admit it. They have also suggested my standards are too low (I liked the mechanic/hunter/libertarian who cursed in every single sentence he uttered) and too high (the baker who was thrilled to talk about going gluten-free, who compared my body to that of a supermodel's—him I didn't want to see again, because he had so many kids, a long commute, and byzantine ice hockey commitments).

My friends claim they can't imagine dating. If their husbands die, they say, they will make it alone. They pat their mates when they say this. They seem not madly in love but madly in small vague terror. I am helping them remember the good parts of marriage after a long, crabby day.

It's funny to me how many of the divorced men from Match.com say to me in conversation, "my wife." How much they talk about the lives from which they have been fired. As though I am a babysitter, guy, shrink, or nice wall.

Fed up with men's ads "seeking women age 18+[one year younger than whatever age they are]," I change my profile. I say I am looking for a man in the age range of eighteen to forty-one; I'm forty-two. But my friend who met the furniture maker says it isn't funny. You can't sound bitter, she says. This isn't the time to make a point.

My friend Ellen met three gorgeous millionaires on Match. All wanted to study Buddhism with her and ride bikes with her; she picked the cyclist from Italy, who is ten years younger and crazy in love with her. "It's not like dating in your twenties," she told me. She says I need to be in my fifties to really do this right. "You're at just the wrong age," she said.

I do not know if dating in my twenties was like dating in my twenties. I was pretending to be a person similar to myself. The pretend person was much better and much worse than my true self. I had no real beliefs.

Almost a year after the start of my coffee project, I've made it to a couple of dozen men.

Number 31 has, he says, simplified his life. "So tell me your life story in twenty words or less," he says, and I do, and he talks for the next twenty-five minutes, leaning forward, elbows on the table: his financial statement, his business plan, his recovery program, four children, his "wife." A man pushing an empty wheelchair can't get past our table. My coffee date doesn't see this, because it is taking place behind him and he is talking to me about the three-million-dollar house in Aspen and how it's good he doesn't have it anymore. I stand up, pull the table a bit. The coffee date sees now, moves chairs. The man pushing the wheelchair still struggles. The chair is like a prop—something he has never seen before, much less used. Finally, he gets past us.

"Do you mind getting the door?" he says to my coffee

date. My coffee date rushes to the door, gallant. "And the next door?" I hear the wheelchair pusher say. They disappear into the foyer. They're gone a long, long time. I sip my water. I finish my salad. I enjoy the time alone. I am thinking: *I can't keep doing this. I want to slip out. I do not want to be rude.*

"People are strange," he says when he comes back. The man with the wheelchair kept asking him to open doors. It was very strange, he said. "He didn't really seem to be going anywhere."

One coffee lasted all winter, and how happy I was on the weekends, playing all that backgammon and keeping score and naming things funny names that meant something to us, skiing, then hunting morels and reading *The Reivers* aloud to each other every night.

It's very distracting, being a loved person. Distracting in a good way. It makes the planet manageable. The planet, which is so large and lonely and blue, and also hurtling through dark empty space. All of which you can feel when you are alone.

I'm not un-whole. I'm not half a person. But being with someone is energizing and relaxing.

I love having a boyfriend. Having a man in one's life is

like having a car in America—easier. A home without a man in it? It gets a little museum-ish. Not bad. Beautiful, and very very very still. Stewarded only by a woman, objects, life, can get weird to the touch, overly pristine.

Like most plans, the plan is pretend. I do *not* want a hundred cups of coffee, a hundred men. I do not want the wrong man. I do not want to be alone. I do not want to do this at all. Yesterday, I doubled down, one at lunch, one at four in the afternoon. Today I am sick in my bed, a summer cold, hell.

Especially good to do with someone one is sleeping with at night: the grocery store, swimming in open water, dog-walking, talking about friends, practicing foreign languages, thinking about houses, riding bikes, breakfast.

Sometimes I feel like a priest, hearing these men confess their lives and wives. Sometimes I feel like an officer of the town of single people. Sometimes I feel like an ambulance chaser, gaping at their stories.

One day I get a trifecta of bad news—my family, my regular life, so many things can go horribly wrong. I call my ex-husband. My dear good friend. Dave and I are divorced, but we are terrible divorced people; we are friendly and helpful to each other and un-mad. We meet at the neighborhood bar, a place I can cry in if need be. Eight, nine years ago, I met this man, my ex-husband now, on Match. He wrote, "I do not know if I could keep up with you, but I know I would enjoy trying." He was the only person I went out with. He was the only person I married.

Then a woman comes into the bar and I recognize her voice; she's a colleague, Joy. I haven't met her boyfriend, and I am happy to now. I introduce my ex, Dave. I happen to know she met her boyfriend on Match. This was years ago. They settle in next to me, happily, and order four appetizers and begin playing the game at the bar, little cards with embarrassing questions.

Then my friend Ellen comes in with her online boyfriend in tow. We hug and carry on. Introductions all around. We sit at the bar facing forward and drink our drinks, man woman, woman man, man woman. I whisper to Dave, "Everyone at this bar met online. Match." He gives me a shocked look. I finish my martini.

Once, I told someone I was the first Match divorce. They were stunned and curious. I was just kidding. I'm sure there were others before me.

Back then, you posted one photo. It scrolled down so

slowly, like a creaky roller blind. He was the first person who wrote me. I wrote him back before his photo finished unrolling. I wrote him back while his forehead was still arriving. He was great right away.

I don't think we look or don't look for love; the heart is a receptor, always working. In spite of our best efforts to protect or hide it. Love looks for us, regardless of how we orient ourselves.

All the coffees have pulled me into human presence, out of myself. The coffees are like Empathy Boot Camp. The coffees remind me of short stories I can't stop thinking about. I have heard forty-one stories of actual lives: lives bungled, misrepresented, frayed, lit by moments of luck or beauty. Lives a lot like my own life. Raw like this, pitched toward me, hope unclenched. I've mostly wanted to run away. I do not even drink coffee.

But I am moving through these coffee shops—Leaf and Bean, Beaners, Cuppe Diem—carefully, a strong, clear woman. And with each sip, I'm closer, I know I am closer, to finding the place in me where love given comes from. And how it is.

Sweet little mysterious sip by sip.

The Love Fast

Rachel Howard

—❦—

I walked into San Francisco's Grace Cathedral on edge, full of worry. It was Ash Wednesday, the first day of Lent. Before I chose to be baptized into the Episcopal Church, in my midtwenties, I hadn't even heard of the holy season of Lent; now it filled me with vague reverence—and befuddlement. In a few minutes I'd kneel at the altar rail, and a priest would draw a smudgy black cross upon my forehead with his thumb, half whispering, *Remember you are dust, and to dust you shall return.* Then would come the forty days of penitence leading up to Easter, and with them a perplexing practice: forty days of fasting.

Fasting confused me because it seemed in theory dark and serious—self-denial, self-punishment—and in action, totally trivial. As far as I could see, most churchgoers gave up something easy like chocolate or red wine, congratulated themselves for going without whatever they didn't really need anyway, and when Easter came, ate Godiva and drank Pinot and went on with their lives as before.

I wanted my life to be different. Church was my ritual, a way to create the stability I still craved two decades after my father's sudden death, and it had gotten me through hard times. A year and a half earlier I'd split from my husband, and now I was rebuilding, finding my own footing. One sign of how I'd moved on: I'd met a smart, kind man and fallen in love.

But there was a catch: Joe squirmed at the slightest emotional pressure. On our third date he professed "commitment issues." Our early courtship was an awkward dance of Joe showering me with affection, then fretting that he couldn't start a relationship, and me reassuring him that he could. It only got worse when he decided he was fully on board. Right away I needed him to tell me he loved me. And though I thought I'd grown so much since leaving my ex—and though I didn't want to torture Joe with the 2:00 A.M. "do you really love me" talks my ex had endured—I still clung to pressure as the only path to reassurance. One night I gazed up at Joe expectantly. "I think you know how I feel about you," I blurted out. "But I'm not sure how you feel about me."

Silence. Joe's face furrowed as my unstated question dawned on him. Over the weeks that followed, even as I watched him flinch, I couldn't get myself to back off. I had a hunch, from the little cakes he kept for me in his refrigerator, from the way he lit up when I arrived at his house, that he did love me. But my need made him resist. His resistance made me apply more pressure. It was hopeless.

Then, on Ash Wednesday, sitting in the pew and worrying about Joe, I was given a new idea of what it means to fast. Fasting, the bishop was saying, didn't have to be about self-denial for its own sake, or giving up some trifle just to feel self-righteous. Traditionally, he continued, the thing people fasted from was food. And the idea was not merely to punish themselves. The idea was that by eating less, those fasting could give the extra food to other people who needed it more. Fasting could be about taking less—in order to give more.

As the bishop's closing words echoed and I knelt and prayed, it came to me. What did I think I needed that I could do with less of? What could I give instead?

Love. I could focus on giving love instead of worrying about how to take it.

So for forty days, I fasted from the need for love. For forty days, I focused on giving love to others. I wrote cards to my grandfather, I called friends and fielded their worries, I smiled more warmly than usual at strangers. I listened to the long story of my hairdresser's harrowing childhood and encouraged him to pursue his dream of going back to college. I devoted a week to helping my brother adjust to civilian life after serving in Iraq.

That part of the discipline came fairly easily. The parts involving Joe did not. Daily I felt the tingling desire to devise some new way of forcing the question. (Aloud: "Don't you think we're wonderful together?" Implied: *Then why can't you say you love me?*) I found myself refusing to offer my love because of fears that he wouldn't return it. I'd withhold a kiss, or fall into a dark mood. But every time I slipped, I returned to my fast. I cleared from my mind the impulse to try to take love. My mood brightened; I kissed him out of spontaneous affection instead of the hope that he'd utter the magic words.

One morning in the middle of my fast, I awoke with a realization: I already had all the love that I needed. I had it from my mother and brother, from my friends, even from the memory of the love that my father had given me before his death. Consciously giving love to others—and seeing them spontaneously give it back—had made me recognize the love in my life more clearly. Most important, I had all the love I needed from God, or whatever you want to call that larger reality of the universe.

I didn't need Joe's love. And yet, I still wanted it.

Near the end of the forty days of Lent, Joe suddenly said, "Perhaps I'm not giving you everything you deserve." We both knew the three unuttered words we were really talking about. He asked to come over, his voice resigned over the crackle of our bad cell phone connection. I had the sad expectation that we would be saying good-bye.

When Joe rang my apartment door, my impulse was to hold myself aloof, to welcome him politely but coolly in case he wasn't, in fact, going to say that he loved me. But then, my arms around him, I thought, *What would happen if I stuck to my fast even now? What if, instead of pulling away because I'm afraid he won't give me love, I stay here holding him, I keep kissing him and letting him feel my love?*

Joe drew back. He said, "I feel overcome by love for you and it feels . . . amazing." And then he said it. "I love you."

It could have gone the other way, of course. Joe could have balked; our relationship could have ended there. My fast from love had prepared me for that possibility—and my acceptance of it made Joe's love possible. The fast continues. As Bishop Marc said at the end of his sermon that Ash Wednesday, if your Lenten fast is a good one, it's not one you ought to give up once the forty days are over. Joe still squirms over commitment. I still fight the urge to pressure him. I'm still tempted, every day, to think I need more love than I already have. And I still feel a strange new peace every time I say "I love you" first.

The Temptations

Susanna Sonnenberg

—❦—

Sex disappeared from my marriage somewhere during our first child's first year. "No big deal," everyone shrugged, "it happens." Laundry, fear, and exhaustion made up my days in a circle spun tightly around the baby. I didn't miss sex, but I missed the person who had loved it.

So tired, my husband and I hardly noticed that with sex gone we also suffered a corrosion of intimacy. I was aware of him only in how he stood too long in the middle of the kitchen when I wanted to pass by to get to the fridge. I experienced his body as a catalog of daily irritations. Our home simmered with polite tension.

The baby grew; we had another. A sort of intimacy crept back as we talked in the dark in bed about our children, but this did not feed into arousal. It was the intimacy of hostages.

One day, waiting by the preschool cubbies, a father brought up piano lessons. I knew Jim from field trips, performances. I hadn't given him much thought—he was too preppy for my taste. But now, as he dropped his voice so as not to disturb the class and leaned into me with his enthusiasm for early musical instruction, I felt the attention of his tone, his look, his breath, as if I had stepped from an air-conditioned office into the sun. His Maine boating clothes made me weak with longing for tidiness, and then, beyond the longing, came the faintest purr of lust. Or rather, something not as youthful and frantic as lust, but the feeling of wanting to feel. *Oh my God*, I thought as he wrote down the name of the instructor, *I want him*.

After about a month, this crush passed, replaced by my crush on Dan, who loved to travel to Europe and talk about good coffee; then came Ted the Republican, Stephen who could build things, Carl who hugged me when I ran into him teaching his kids how to bike. None of these men thought about me nursing when they looked at me. None saw someone half-asleep and miserable. They saw, even though they didn't know it, the someone who used to be there.

Sometime just after my crush on Matt (who coached Little League), my husband was standing at the sink, filling a glass. I looked at the rightness of his shoulders, felt pleased when he said the words I knew he was thinking. He turned around and I teased him, almost meeting his eye in a feigned gesture of high school flirtation. He put his arm around my middle, that's all, but the spread of lust warmed my thighs, my fingertips, and I thought, *I want him.*

Yes, him. My husband. Each crush had revived a dormant element of that girl, had undone the stays of maternal duty just a bit. My husband and I hadn't known, on the eve of parenthood eight years ago, that children, money, and hormones would figure so prominently in our sex life, weren't aware of their combined deadly effect. But we also had no idea back then what power we would bank by sharing life.

Looking Out for No. 2

Lise Funderberg

—❦—

It wasn't until I decided to marry again that I realized how completely uncertain and illogical marriage is. The second time around, you can't hide behind romantic innocence. You already know how easy it is to take another person for granted. You know how hard it is to live with someone else: to build intimacy over years, to grow without stealing all the available sunlight and food, or to simply like that other person day in and day out despite chore wars, seat-up/seat-down debates, and other domestic disputes such as appropriate use of mayonnaise in sandwich-making (never versus always). The second time around, you already know how easy it is to fail.

Forget corroborating statistics (divorce for almost

50 percent of first marriages and 40 percent of second); anyone can see that failure lurks on the other side of the next financial downturn or conflict in life directions or mountain of careless, bruising words. All around, marriages are crumbling, families are splintering, people are retreating into corners, making do, putting up, shutting off.

And yet even before I met John, even as I combed through the ashes of the first marriage, looking for what to discard and what to salvage, I realized the idea of marriage didn't repel me. The problem had been in thinking that it marked the arrival at a destination instead of signaling a point of departure. It wasn't marriage that had failed my first husband and me: By expecting it to maintain itself based on one sunny April afternoon of exchanged vows, we had failed it.

In divorce's aftermath, people, friends, and acquaintances seemed to anticipate bitterness—they expected bile and brokenness when sharing the news of other people's nuptials. They got neither. I had a greater respect for the institution. I was humbled by the enterprise I had come to see as demanding courage and hope and a relentless investment of self. I was in awe.

When John and I both recognized the irreversible pull

between us—the astounding affinity, the willingness to understand, the tenderness, the fun—we started to consider a future. We fit as a couple; we fit in the larger context of each other's lives. He actually liked my eccentric family, the forces of nature that they can be. And I was crazy about his seventeen-year-old son, who lived with him and who stepped off the path of adolescent individuation rites long enough to allow me glimpses of his kind heart and sharp mind, as well as a chance to find my way around that phenomenon I'd never understood—the teenage boy.

John and I shared a striking number of interests (urban living, pork) and traits (bossiness, get-up-and-go). What we didn't share we admired, and what we didn't admire we accepted. My brilliant therapist had been telling me all along that a mature love is one in which the beloved can have flaws but still be considered a perfect match. Oh, I thought, I get it now.

After two years of tumbling and inching toward each other, John and I married—in my (now our) backyard, with 150 witnesses and 40 slabs of barbecued ribs, a mess of side dishes where a first marriage's gift table might have been, and a feeling of pleasure that was quiet and sure. In front of a village of loved ones we pledged our troth, and I felt with equal conviction that I (a) was doing the right thing and (b) had no idea what I was getting into.

The paradox of those realizations prompted what John calls a BFO: a blinding flash of the obvious. Suddenly, I understood that marriage is, as it has often been said, a leap of faith. I had just made the leap; now came the faith. In that moment, I saw that my best hope for defying statistics and building a strong union was to consider marriage a spiritual act that requires devotion and practice and the same naked honesty that people seek between themselves and their god(s).

I am not religious in the conventional sense, certainly not what some of my relatives would call churched. I grew up in a religious minority's minority, a birthright Unitarian, and in my adulthood I have—if it's possible for Unitarians to do so—lapsed. But I attend weddings and funerals and civil commitments, baby dedications and bat mitzvahs, and any number of holidays and ceremonies. My Methodist, African Methodist, and Colored Methodist relatives have not left the church, and so I have had the opportunity over the years to witness the faith of others, a stirring and beautiful thing.

Among the friends and relations whose spirituality I

admire, I've noted that their practice is not restricted to a particular day of the week, but applied to the twists and turns of everyday life. Likewise, my commitment to this marriage is not something I dust off at anniversaries or in the wake of troubles. It is a close and constant touchstone. I am conscious of this promise I've made to John to cast my lot with his, to be a guardian of his unguarded heart as I offer up my own.

Consciousness introduces a higher plane on which to relate, retreat, take solace, and find answers, to rise above the petty fray. Unfortunately, it's not a complete guarantee against quotidian tangles. It would still kill no one to put the toilet seat back down, to know where the vacuum is stored and act upon said knowledge. Or to remember that he has more than once explained to me in assiduous detail the virtues of the Norton 850 Commando, which was one of the fastest production motorcycles you could buy in 1973, when European motorcycles still dominated the market for performance and before Japan's Honda 750 four-cylinder hit and immediately took over.

Faith demands belief in what you can't see. I know, for example, that I must have my own version of the Norton Commando story, even if I'm unaware of it. And believing that allows me to be more patient. When John goes on about some great passion of his that I rank up there with paint drying and software downloading, I remind myself that this is an opportunity I'm being given to challenge my own limits, that it is a gift to share in someone else's enthusiasm and imagination, and that this is what happens when you live with someone day after day after day. If all else fails, I use the time to reflect on last spring's trip to France, how perfect the weather was, how wonderful it was to rummage through country flea markets together, and how we kept our sense of humor when all the charming hotels were booked during the week of the Ascension and we ended up in a bland motor inn overlooking a big-box mall.

Faith is a way to step outside yourself, to remember that this anecdote, too, shall pass; that being a team is more important than which exit he takes off the highway; that you don't need to balance the checkbook the same way in order to prove that you're evenly yoked and well suited; and that annoyance and blame are often the result of misplaced anxieties, which, if clearly identified, could most likely be addressed and resolved without leaving open or festering wounds. We are all, as the psychotherapist Deborah

Luepnitz writes, porcupines. We seek the warmth of others but soon tangle ourselves in one another's prickly quills.

Faith, among the faithful I know, is not about perfection. It's about knowing, as Quakers would put it, that there is an inextinguishable light inside everyone that is holy. It's about valuing the holy in the face of the flawed, about leaving room to grow, to fall down, then get back up again, all with equal dignity. And so, I find after some practice, is a good marriage.

Dead Reckoning

Meg Giles

—❦—

I sit in an SUV on East Main Street in Scottsdale, Arizona, 11.2 miles from my father, who is in a hospital in Phoenix; 8.2 miles from the cemetery where my mother is buried; 4.2 miles from the home where I grew up, which must be sold to pay my father's debts; 2,398 miles from my husband, two daughters, job, friends, and home, all in New York City; and two feet from a man I've loved for twenty years. We speak about regretting leaving each other long ago.

"Why didn't you ask me to stay?" I say.

"I didn't know it was an option." He sighs. "Can I have you in the next lifetime?"

We are in our forties. We live in different cities, belong

to others, and are parents to, between us, seven kids. It would be impossible—*impossible*—to change course.

Yet somehow I find myself saying, "Fuck the next lifetime. I am going to die someday."

I'm perfectly healthy. According to the actuarial table, I'm unlikely to die for another forty years. But death has been on my mind, flashing in my periphery. I once looked at a diving board and thought, "I wonder if I've already done my last front flip." I was thirty-six. I couldn't stand the idea. So I did one then and have done one every summer since. There will come a day when my aging body will prevent me from doing another. But today isn't that day.

In navigation, dead reckoning is the process of calculating a position relative to a previous point. The exact places where we make our decisions usually go unmarked. But in the signal moments of my life, death has served as my own personal North Star.

One such moment is right now in this SUV. Sitting beside Carlos, I take my bearings: I have a good marriage, not a passionate one. I work for people I admire and adore, but my job is ending. I live in a glamorous city, but long for fewer bills, better sleep, proximity to my father, and space for my kids. In that driver's seat, I make a choice:

I'm not interested in the next lifetime. I will live in this one.

I change my return flight, extending my stay in Phoenix another two weeks. I want a chance to explore a love whose loss I have always mourned, a chance to help my father, a chance to pause. I ask myself, "If the last stop on my trip is death, what do I want to do, to feel, between now and then?" Between this point and death, I want to make love to this man. Between this point and death, I need a marriage full of ardor instead of bonhomie. Between this point and death, I don't want to be too shy or too safe.

Carlos says, "I've drawn half my breaths in this life." We've lost twenty years. We don't want to lose more. I return to New York and quit my job. I leave my husband. I move with my girls to Phoenix. My friend David writes an e-mail: "Carpe diem, yes, fine, sure. But why are we behaving as if we all have six months left to live?"

But why behave as if I have sixty years?

I try to sell my father's house, but can't do it. I want it: the quail, the olive tree, the big eucalyptus, the jackrabbits. I want to watch my girls run down the same hallway I did. I buy the house from my father, move in, and ask Carlos and his kids to move in, too. To others it seems reckless; to us it seems overdue. My soon-to-be ex-husband thinks I'm not in my right mind. David says that after fifteen years, he can no longer bear being my friend. My sister bursts into tears and asks if this isn't all "a little too soon." And I wonder if I've gone too far. If I will live to regret this. If I've broken my husband's heart, derailed my daughters. I feel alone and adrift and half the time insane. To make this leap, I need a faith that's almost religious—in my instincts, my desire, this man, and myself. But a friend tells me: "Love expands." And for that, there is plenty of evidence. My life grows emphatically richer. I suddenly have *more*—people, space, joy. More heartache, for certain. But that's life, and I have more of that now, too.

When I'm not despairing, I see that what I have is extraordinary. Carlos and I wake each morning in the house where I grew up, in the room where my mother drew her last breath. The sun peeks through the glass doors. Jackrabbits nibble the grass. Quail dart along the deck. The olive tree stands sentry. Soon the kids will pile into bed with us. Carlos says, "We have another day." There will come a morning when I will have done my last front flip, inhaled my children for the last time, made love to Carlos for the last time. There will come a day when one of us isn't in that bed, when we will have had each and every one of our days. He makes a wedding ring for me from the olive tree my mom planted outside our bedroom. I say hell yes. Death is the ultimate destination, no matter which way I steer. And I want to live days worth dying for.

Ends and Beginnings

I remembered that the real world was wide, and
that a varied field of hopes and fears, of sensations
and excitements, awaited those who had courage
to go forth into its expanse . . .

—CHARLOTTE BRONTË, *JANE EYRE*

When the Heart Stays Open

Elizabeth Lesser

It seems it's human nature to resist change, to run around like two-year-olds saying *NO! NO! NO!* when things show up that we didn't order. But hard things are hard enough to deal with on their own; adding a tantrum only makes them harder.

My beloved younger sister died recently after a long battle with cancer. Every time I feel the tide of *NO* rising in my heart, I catch myself. I sit down, close my eyes, put my hand on my chest, breathe, and whisper *YES*. Yes, this happened. Yes, I can face it. Yes, I will feel the loss and not fight the grief.

Because unexpected gifts are given when the heart

stays open. I've found that the changes I feared would ruin me have always become doorways, and on the other side I have found a more courageous and graceful self.

Second Wind

Lee Montgomery

—❧—

Last summer I spent my days—every last one—in the Columbia River Gorge. I watched the water's surface ripple like crumpled paper; sometimes the wind blew 25 miles an hour, sometimes 30, with gusts in the 40s. And then I waded in, day in, day out, in my wetsuit, helmet, and harness, carrying my windsurfing board, knowing the river would hand my ass to me just like it had the day before.

The Columbia is the body of water that divides much of Washington and Oregon, and enthusiasts count it among the best windsurfing locales in the world. For good windsurfers, it's paradise. But I am not a good windsurfer. I'd lift my sail, and a gust would rip it from my hands. I would try again, sometimes popping up on the board, hooking into the harness, slipping my foot into the strap, but the wind was often so strong that the board would levitate and I'd find myself airborne, then flung forward and trapped underwater.

Though my friends struggled to understand what I was doing, taking on the gorge was about recovering—from twenty-five years of crazy ambition that had wreaked havoc on my life. I'd been elevated, then ruined. Powered up, mowed down. I'm it; I'm shit. After a decade at the publishing company I'd helped establish and run, I was fired—on my tenth anniversary. Two weeks before Christmas. Via e-mail.

In other words, getting my ass handed to me had become something of a theme in my life.

I had worked so hard for so long. I was always doing something—breathlessly, relentlessly, furiously writing, editing, hanging with friends in high places, clawing my way up the ladder. And so what? Doing these things had netted me, in the end, very little of lasting value. I wondered what would happen if I let it all go—didn't look for a job, didn't keep mainlining ambition.

My husband thought it was a great idea. "Just stop," he said. "Refill the well." A serious windsurfer, he suggested

I try the sport as a path to clarity. (He always joked that windsurfing was like putting a leaf blower to your brain.) I am fifty-six years old, twenty pounds overweight (again), and have had back surgery for two ruptured disks. I had windsurfed before, but only in calm water. I didn't like high winds. I didn't like going fast.

But I wanted to abandon the past. I wanted to feel the fear and do it anyway. I wanted to learn how to ride the currents, to stay nimble, to lean into whatever came—and I couldn't think of a better way than to devote myself to the invisible, ever-shifting wind. After all, as the cliché goes, weren't the winds of change upon me?

Using the wind as a path toward transformation was not a new idea—ancient spiritual teachings are full of exhortations to emulate it. The *I Ching* counsels that we need to bend like bamboo in the wind without being broken. The Tao says we cannot see the wind but we can observe its force, the way it changes things. The wind powers journeys, moves seeds, enables rebirth. That last one sounded pretty good to me.

I decided to sail at Swell City, a favorite outpost on the Washington side of the Columbia, where a small contingent of sailors spend most of their waking hours sailing, smoking pot, and drinking beers. Rock 'n' roll blared from trucks and beater vans. Everyone had a nickname: Wolfie. Fucking Dave. Buddha Stan. ChooChoo John. Suzy Hot-Bod. There was good-natured ribbing, and impromptu barbecues, and endless talk about the wind: where it is, where it will be, what it will be doing.

That July turned out to be one of the windiest months on record. The hot, gusty days blurred into one another. The sheer physical effort of the act was addictive. And out in the middle of the mighty Columbia, I remained capti-vated by its beauty. The snowy hat of Mount Hood looked down from the distance. Egrets and bald eagles dive-bombed for salmon. I marveled: What I was doing accom-plished nothing for anyone. It did nothing for my standing in the world. It won me no friends. No admirers. There were only endless reaches of back and forth, the wind and the water, the sky and me beneath it.

A lot of the time I was terrified. When the winds went wild, I was too frightened to hook into my harness because in powerful gusts I'd be thrown into the air, tethered to my sail. The whole system depended on a series of con-nections: mast to board, harness to person. So when strong winds blew, I'd bounce on the board, holding on for dear life, or get mowed down by the swell. Other sailors were dumbfounded: Why fight the wind?

"Gotta hook in," they'd say. "Gotta go faster."

I also couldn't jibe, which is to turn around, swinging the rig over the front of the board. You have to sail fast, commit wholly, and lean forward into nothingness to drive the board through the turn before flipping the sail in front of you. It's a masterful move that combines speed, power, grace, and timing, and separates the casual sailor from the expert. It seemed impossible to nail. But it was also an apt metaphor for what I needed to do in my life.

So again and again, I did the thing I dreaded: I went fast. Committed wholly. Leaned into nothingness. I sailed until I was exhausted. And I kept going. That summer I broke two toes. My arms ached. My legs, covered in bruises, spasmed at night. And I was happier than I ever remembered being.

I sailed by day, and my psyche went to work at night. I dreamed about bridges crumbling beneath my feet, being tied up with rope, cars unable to accelerate up hills. But every morning I'd awake to the possibility of the jibe, imagining my feet steering the board, my hands pulling up the sail, flipping, catching. Turn around! Turn around! After two hot, glorious months, I still couldn't jibe—but I learned something just as crucial.

One day a friend and her fifteen-year-old son came out to the Gorge with me, and after I explained my trials, my long and fruitless journey toward the jibe, he said the simplest, most profound thing: "It's all in the attitude." This kid had been windsurfing exactly three times, yet he knew the secret. "If you go out there knowing you're going to rock it, you will," he continued. "But if you go out there afraid you'll get hurt, you will."

I smiled at him. Wasn't that precisely the same problem I'd encountered in life? I'd always been terrified I wouldn't reach the goal, make the grade, land the job or the contract or the deal—and sure enough, I'd watched my worst professional fear come true.

I knew I had to let that fear go. And slowly I did. Even after a particularly bad day of flailing, when I vowed I would never, ever windsurf again, if the wind went up the next day I'd be back at it, driven by the insane memories of the spectacular days when everything clicked perfectly and pure magic took over. Powered by the wind, fully locked and loaded, you push your legs out and hang out over the water, steer with your toes and heels, flying weightless, carried by the elements. There is no other feeling like it in the world.

The wind wanted nothing from me. It cared not at all about my ambition, my accomplishments. It reminded me that the beauty of life is in the trying, day after day. And that's where I am: still trying for the turnaround, in life and in the wind.

A Rose Is a Rose
Is a Miracle Cure

Helen Oyeyemi

—⟨❧⟩—

The winter of 2010 was hard on my heart. There was a man
I could have really fallen for—I was on the brink of loving
him madly, out of all measure. Once, thinking of the fact
that I was due to be with him in a few days' time, I took a
stick of solid perfume and wrote his name along my left
arm, watching the pale strokes melt as I formed them, the
large letters crossing the visible vein in my wrist. As for
his opinion of me, he didn't mind my company, but he
wouldn't go out of his way to seek it; one night in London
he said he'd like to see me whenever I next found myself
in town. I lived in Prague. I might not have taken it quite
so hard if it hadn't been for the three other non-romances

I'd already had that year. I'd felt less for those, but four hollow affairs in a row were too many.

I gave up on the year, made a note to myself to reset on January 1, and just after Christmas turned my attention to a trip I'd been planning since the summer, when I won a UK prize for young writers. The award was instituted by the late Somerset Maugham and given with the stipulation that the prize money be spent on foreign travel. From a friend I learned that Angela Carter had used her 1969 windfall to free herself from an unhappy marriage and move to Japan, where she became a radical feminist and fell in lust with a local man. From a Web site I learned that Kingsley Amis reluctantly used his 1955 award on a trip to Portugal, then wrote a novel about the indignities of traveling abroad.

I chose Istanbul, out of a desire to know something of a city one of my favorite writers, Agatha Christie, had passed through many times. When I booked my ticket, I was wholly unaware that heartbreak would be my travel companion.

By the time I arrived, my senses were in deep hibernation and preferred not to be disturbed. I was so sad that I felt a lean in my center of gravity as I walked—my progress over the paved stones was unsteady, as if there were water in my ear canal. I dropped off my bags at a bed-and-breakfast and made for the Pera Palace Hotel in Beyoglu, where Christie is said to have written part of *Murder on the Orient Express*.

The surroundings were sumptuous, but there was a sinister smallness, too, as if the grand hotel had shrunk over time and soon nothing would be left but a shriveled, gold-coated claw. I took afternoon tea in a curved Turkish glass and ignored the cakes and sandwiches, which seemed to be purely decorative. I'd brought Somerset Maugham's *Of Human Bondage* with me and became better acquainted with the protagonist, who in his boyhood believed in hell more than heaven because it seemed to him that anguish could last longer than life, and happiness most likely could not.

I remembered the first time I heard the *adhan*, the call to prayer, in the Alabaster Mosque in Cairo, which I'd visited in 2004 after reading that Malcolm X had prayed there once. I'd sat cross-legged on the richly patterned carpet, and this sound came ringing through the white pillars that encircled all of us in the main body of the mosque, a sound of such longing and such clarity that, at nineteen years old, I thought it came from inside myself. Now, in Istanbul, muezzins recited the *adhan* five times a day from hundreds of minarets in the sky, their messages to the faithful flowing over the rooftops and pooling around transfixed foreigners like me.

Looking out across Istanbul from the Galata Bridge, I saw its history, with part of the city situated in Europe and the other part in Asia. I watched the Bosphorus flow between the continents. On both sides, stoic fishermen baited and slung hooks for hours throughout the day. Women in burqas took tea with bareheaded girls in jeans. Headscarves matched up with minidresses and colorful tights. I observed all this as if through a screen. When people spoke to me I felt surprised and slightly reproachful, as if I'd been watching a black-and-white thriller and one of the characters suddenly turned to me for advice.

At night, in a darkened room above a quiet street, musicians in white robes played the *baglama* and the oud, and dervishes whirled and cast shadows on the brilliantly lit squares beneath their feet. The nakedness of their ecstasy was so shocking, I couldn't look at the Sufis' faces. Instead, I watched their hands, which, beginning at waist level, slowly, slowly rose as their arms were pulled up above their heads, as if unfurling, extending toward divine love that returned in waves and soaked them to the core. They made me feel, for the first time, that I might never find the kind of love I need. Still, the presence of those joyful dancers made it impossible to do the sensible thing and give up hope.

The next day, December 31, I visited Topkapi Palace, home to generations of Ottoman sultans. The palace is a fantasy of wealth and power. Topkapi is a place of tall trees, hidden windows, and luxurious prisons—living quarters for eunuchs and slave girls kidnapped from all over the world. I saw its beauty, but the nature of that beauty was entirely cruel. Shameless city, beckoning my imagination with its ancient intrigues and rococo seaside mosques. I was wary of a seduction that would lead nowhere.

Hours later, at Hagia Sophia, I stared up at the weathered mosaics depicting Christ and his mother alongside the names of Allah and Muhammad, among others, written in green and gold, and it came to me that I was standing in one of the wonders of the world. I couldn't even manage a smile. That night I lay on my stomach in bed, stuck on a single sentence of Maugham's novel: "Sometimes he felt so lonely that he could not read...." At midnight, as the year turned, I thought I heard fireworks, and went to the window to find that it was celebratory gunfire. Youths with rifles, laughing.

In the morning I ate a filling meal, almost for novelty purposes. When you're unhappy and trying to conceal it, eating or drinking anything with any flavor constitutes a risk—there's no telling what might make you cry. But I was flying west to the archaeological site of Ephesus later that morning, to wander amid the rubble of the goddess Artemis' ruined city, and I thought I'd better have some sweetness first. There was some jam in a dish on the table, and I poured a spoonful of it over my yogurt. I thought it was strawberry jam, but it wasn't. Rose petals hung suspended in the thickness of the syrup, some soft, some crisp with crystallized sugar, and the taste...the wistful, earthy bloom of it on my tongue made me think of Narnia, the fragrant pull of the Turkish Delight that Edmund betrayed his siblings to taste.

Later that day at Ephesus, I saw the most innocent-looking Judas trees growing around the broken shell of the Library of Celsus, and olive trees hanging their branches over the roofs of doorless stone houses, and realized there was a change in the way I was seeing. A subtle change that needed nursing, but it was there, and it was real. I'd just had flowers for breakfast, so I put the effect down to that.

On my return to Istanbul, I began to investigate the many uses of the rose. At the Spice Bazaar in Eminönü I bought rose clay soap, attar of roses, dried rosebuds for tea, and more rose petal jam, all made from the pink damask roses from Isparta that Turkey is so rightly proud of. The clear oil distilled from the petals of those mountain roses is said to be worth its weight in gold. In the days that followed, I was reminded why roses have been exchanged by lovers for so many hundreds of years. I went out into the city wearing invisible dots of rose oil—one on each wrist, and another in the notch at the center of my collarbone. At night I brought the scent of rose clay soap into bed with me, warm, but slightly dark, a whispered reminder of thorns.

The fragrance of roses is vertical—over the course of a day it gets deeper and richer until, quite suddenly, you've reached the final layer, and it's gone. Little by little, there in my Istanbul bed of roses, my emotions fell back into their natural order. I slept calmly, without dreams.

However awful the storm of my disappointment, it's a response that belongs to me. It's my heart, after all. My territory, my kingdom. And since I'm the only one with the authority to surrender it, I can also take it back. The retraction is painful, of course, but it comes in handy when yearning for the wrong someone.

And at the low points before you're ready to recover, when you feel something in you so wild, something like a sob you could never have enough breath to let out, when sleep does nothing for you and music makes things worse, I recommend accepting the friendship of roses: They promise the fulfillment of desire but don't have an air of laughter about them the way other flowers do. The rose commands (that's why it's sometimes called the sultan of flowers). It is solemn and insistent until you answer that you'll wait faithfully for what you want.

There's a couplet of Rumi's that struck me years ago, though I didn't quite grasp its imperative tone at the time. Now I think he might have written it like that because this is just how it happens:

"With friends, say only mystery.

Near roses, sing."

Dog Rest His Soul

Trish Deitch

—❦—

I have always been proud of the fact that my daughter wouldn't hurt a fly. At twelve, she went camping with other Buddhist kids along Colorado's Cache la Poudre River, and they spent an evening clearing a tent of marauding mosquitoes without killing a single one. They chanted a mantra that purifies negative karma—*om mani padme hum*—while using plastic cups to bail each vile creature, filled with the kids' own blood, out into the night air.

Some Buddhists believe that if you end an animal's life before its karma has run its natural course, its suffering could, in the next life, be much worse. I believe in karma and rebirth, and for many years thought that I, too, wouldn't hurt a fly. And then one day I found myself at the vet's office, asking him to kill my dog.

Scout, whom I'd raised from a fat-bellied pig of a pup, used to run joyfully and fast with the neighborhood boys, who'd knock on our door to ask whether he could come out to play. He was so smart and funny that I always felt that, like Pinocchio, he was *this close* to being a real boy. But when he was ten years old, he started peeing in the house. Overnight he went deaf. It turned out he had a brain tumor.

I told myself euthanasia was not an option, and for the next year or so fed Scout by hand, carried him up and down the stairs in the middle of the night and washed his paws when he pooped in the house and circled in it, which he did constantly—circling and circling, nose to tail, night and day. He wore a raw patch in the pad of his pivoting foot.

There came a night when Scout's circling turned frantic. He spun so fast, he knocked his head against a doorjamb and fell with a bony crash—only to scramble up to keep circling, his eyes wild. I called two vets, who both said that soon Scout would start convulsing, and the convulsions would never end. He'd have to be put into a coma to stop them, and he'd stay in the coma until he died. That I couldn't bear.

So I went to the second vet, a gentle man who understood that what I was doing went against every belief I had. He sat on the floor with me while Scout received two injections: one to calm him and the other to stop his heart. I expected to be able to say good-bye before the second injection, but Scout collapsed in my arms after the first one, a weight so heavy and still, he seemed already dead. And then, a minute later, he *was* dead.

I thought I would feel one thing—the sorrow of having violated my beliefs—but I felt something else entirely. I felt that Scout had been liberated from his painful, creaky, used-up body and was out in the space above me, free. I felt him once again as my joyful, graceful, leaping boy. It was a relief, this bright, surprising vision, where I'd expected only a void.

Still, I cried all the way back from the vet's office and for two days after, like a faucet that couldn't be turned off. I could function fine, but as I went about my business, the tears rained down my face. Part of the crying was grief, of course—that sweet dog had made me happy—but it also felt like a cleansing: Whatever feelings came up, they flowed out with the tears. That had never happened to me before, such an easy current of feeling. The crying felt good.

Not wanting my attachment to Scout and his things to keep him here, I gathered up his squeaky toys and his dolls, his collar and his bed, and put them all in a large black garbage bag. I cried as I swept up fur from the floor and vacuumed dirt and grass from the seams of the couch. Down on my hands and knees, salty, snotty rivulets streaming, I scrubbed little patches of dried blood with steel wool and sponged tiny black dog hairs from behind the toilet. When I was done, I put everything of Scout's in the trunk of my car and drove it to the dump.

I have always held on so tight: to the loss, to the lover, to the love. But now I saw that grasping—even of dearly held beliefs—causes us and others needless pain. Everything is constantly flowing and changing. Nothing and no one lasts. The best gift we can give ourselves and those we love is to let them be part of the nature of things: the raging river, the growing child, the dying light.

Out of the Darkness

Emily Rapp Black

—❦—

When I learned that I was pregnant last year, I felt joy, and then panic that mounted daily. I struggled to sleep. I was distracted at work. Even when I wasn't nauseated, food had no appeal. Although an inevitable part of parenting is to be liquefied with terror that some calamity might befall your child, for me, the stress was unrelenting. My pregnancy was closely monitored at a fertility clinic, which somehow made the panic more acute. Was this ache or that twinge normal? I called the nurse multiple times a day. My therapist encouraged me to relax and live in the moment, but this was proving impossible.

I knew what it was like to lose a child. My son, Ronan, was born with Tay-Sachs disease, a rare neurological disorder with no cure. For two agonizing years after his diagnosis, he slowly regressed into a vegetative state; at age three, when he could no longer swallow, he died. I'd tried everything to cope with the heartache: meditation, running, yoga, slamming heavy ropes onto the floor. My grief was a full-body experience that I had to work through both psychologically and physically. But while some of the techniques helped for a bit, they were no longer giving me relief. How could I parent a new child if I was in a constant state of dread?

In the final weeks of his life, I'd booked Ronan a massage-like treatment called Core Synchronism. The idea is that every bone, muscle, and organ "opens" and "closes" as a core current of cerebrospinal fluid runs clockwise through our bodies. When the current runs freely, these movements are synchronized, reducing emotional and physical pain and distress. By manipulating the fluid that moves our bodily structures, proponents believe, Core Synchronism gets all our parts moving together in harmony. Even I, who was willing to try anything, was skeptical, but after the treatment, Ronan perked up and felt less tense in my arms. Now I wondered if the same practitioner could help me, too.

I remained fully clothed on a fold-up massage table while the woman placed her palms on my head, back, neck, legs, feet, and face, holding them for a few seconds or several long minutes until she felt each part "synchronize." For an hour, I didn't feel much apart from the soothing warmth of her hands, but when she was finished, I was calm and strangely vibrant. I became newly aware of my body: the feel of a chair against my back, the hair on my neck. It was as if my internal warning mechanism, after two and a half years of grinding fear, had finally relaxed. I felt warm all over, as if I'd been sleeping in the sun.

I worked up the nerve to ask a question: "What did you feel with Ronan?"

Months before, I'd been afraid to know. Now she told me she'd felt his body at peace but shutting down, his spirit winding counterclockwise toward the end, unraveling.

"And what do you feel now?" I asked.

Her answer: two forces spinning strongly clockwise, mine and my daughter's, circling toward life.

How We Want to Live

Kathleen Volk Miller

—❦—

Thirteen summers ago, my family and I went to the fireworks show in our small New Jersey town. We were so close
to where they were shooting them off that we had to lie on
our backs to see. The lights rained down upon us, bits of
paper falling onto our faces. I started to panic. What about
the kids' hearing? What chemicals were we breathing in?
I looked at my husband. His face told me he had the same
concerns, but we were in it now, so we might as well go with
it. The kids squealed when the ash landed on their little
bodies, and our middle child reached out her chubby hand
and yelled, "I so happy, Mommy!" And I knew she was, and
I was, too.

Four months later, my husband was diagnosed with a

carcinoid cancer, a rare form we were told was "manage-able." Nine months later, he died. In his final weeks the doctors kept saying he'd pull through, so I told my children the same thing. In May, while he lay in the hospital in a medicated coma, I assured them we'd be fishing in the Po-conos by August.

The morning their father died, I called the kids to the couch and made sure I was touching each one. When I gave them the news, my oldest screamed, "You're lying!" The other two, sobbing, said, "You said we were going fish-ing! You said we were going to the Poconos!"

Relatives and friends took over the house, bringing food and flowers, wanting to do the impossible, which was make us feel better. But finally, it was just us, sitting at the table in our new configuration. We left Dad's seat empty. It was mid-June, and summer loomed ahead.

"You guys," I said. "The most horrible thing that can happen to a family has happened to us. There's nothing I can say or do to make that less true. But we have a choice. We can pull down the blinds and stay here and just be. Or we can be thankful for our friends and family and each other. We can go to the beach. We can still have a summer. We have to decide how we want to live."

Hayley, eleven years old, said, "I choose the second thing. Let's have fun. But can we still think about Dad, too?"

Allison, thirteen years old, said, "Of course we can think about Dad. But he wouldn't mind if we had a summer."

Christopher, our baby, was five. He said, "Let's not stay inside with the windows shut, except when we have to."

We agreed. Let's stay inside only on days we have to.

It turned out that sadness didn't last whole days, just parts of days. Allison watched videos of her dad late at night and cried body-wracking sobs. Hayley stormed around, making demands: "What are we going to do now? What's for dinner? Can we go to the mall?" Chris lay in bed with the 8×10 of his dad carrying him on his shoulders. He would weep, not wanting me to remove the photo, but also not wanting to look at it.

We didn't bother with blind optimism or denial—we were all keenly aware of what we had lost. Instead, we approached every hour with the aim to take from it the best we could. One day we were in the car when "Hey Ya!" by Outkast came on the radio. It seemed to be everywhere that summer and was impossible not to dance to. So we did: Windows down, radio up, we sang loud and bounced hard. A few blocks from home, a neighbor on the corner watched us pass with a look of abject horror. Here we were, so publicly happy, though my husband, their father, was only six weeks gone.

The neighbor didn't understand how joy could exist in the midst of tragedy. To be honest, neither do I. But it can. It did. And we were grateful.

Contributors

Katie Arnold-Ratliff is the articles editor at *O, The Oprah Magazine* and the author of the novel *Bright Before Us*.

Martha Beck, Ph.D., is a life coach whose monthly column has appeared in *O, The Oprah Magazine* since 2001. She is the author most recently of *Diana, Herself: An Allegory of Awakening*, as well as the bestselling *Finding Your Own North Star* and *Expecting Adam. The Martha Beck Collection: Essays for Creating Your Right Life*, Volume 1, is an anthology of her work from *O*.

Molly Birnbaum's 2011 memoir, *Season to Taste: How I Lost My Sense of Smell and Found My Way*, was shortlisted for an International Association of Culinary Professionals award in Literary Food Writing. Her work has appeared in the *New York Times*, *Modern Farmer*, and *Fast Company*. She is the executive editor of *Cook's Science* at America's Test Kitchen and lives in Providence, Rhode Island.

Emily Rapp Black is the author of *Poster Child: A Memoir* and *The Still Point of the Turning World*, which was a *New York Times* bestseller and a finalist for the PEN Center Literary Award in Nonfiction. An assistant professor of creative writing at the University of California-Riverside, she has written for a number of publications, including *Vogue*, *The Los Angeles Times*, and *The Wall Street Journal*.

Amy Bloom has written three novels, including the bestsellers *Lucky Us* and *Away;* three collections of short stories; a children's book; and a collection of essays. She has been nominated for both the National Book Award and the National Book Critics Circle Award, and won a National Magazine Award for Fiction; her stories have appeared in *Best American Short Stories, Prize Stories: The O. Henry Awards*, and numerous anthologies. Currently she is Wesleyan University's Distinguished Writer-in-Residence.

Sarah Broom's essays have appeared in *The New Yorker*, *The New York Times Magazine*, and *The Oxford American*, among other publications. Her memoir, *The Yellow House*, is forthcoming from Grove Press. She lives in upstate New York.

Kelly Corrigan is the author of *The New York Times* bestsellers *Lift*, *Glitter and Glue*, and *The Middle Place*. She lives in San Francisco with her husband and two daughters.

Trish Deitch has written articles and essays for a publications including *Elle*, *New York*, *The New York Times*, and *The Los Angeles Times*. She has been a fiction editor at *GQ*, the blogs editor at *The New Yorker*, an executive editor at the *Shambhala Sun* and *Tricycle*, and a story editor for the filmmaker Sydney Pollack.

Junot Díaz received a 2008 Pulitzer Prize for his novel *The Brief Wondrous Life of Oscar Wao*. His other books include the short-story collections *This Is How You Lose Her* and *Drown*. He is a professor of writing at MIT.

Caitlin Flanagan is a contributing editor to *The Atlantic*. She has been cancer-free for seven years, and her sons graduated from high school in June 2016.

Bonnie Friedman is the author of the bestselling and widely anthologized *Writing Past Dark: Envy, Fear, Distraction, and Other Dilemmas in the Writer's Life*. Her latest book is *Surrendering Oz: A Life in Essays*.

Lise Funderburg has contributed to publications ranging from *The New York Times Magazine* to *National Geographic*. She is the author of the books *Pig Candy: Taking My Father South, Taking My Father Home*; and *Black, White, Other: Biracial Americans Talk About Race and Identity*. She lives in Philadelphia with her husband of fourteen years.

Meg Giles is a writer who lives in Scottsdale, Arizona, with her husband, her kids, and her dog, Quixote.

Rachel Howard lives with her husband and daughter in the Sierra Nevada foothills of California. She is a fiction writer, an arts journalist, and the author of *The Lost Night*, a memoir about the emotional aftermath of her father's unsolved murder.

Elizabeth Lesser is the cofounder of The Omega Institute and the author of three books, including, most recently, the memoir *Marrow: A Love Story*.

Suzanne McMinn is the author of *Chickens in the Road: An Adventure in Ordinary Splendor*. Her Web site is chickensintheroad.com.

Maile Meloy has written two novels, *Liars and Saints* and *A Family Daughter*, and the story collections *Half in Love* and *Both Ways Is the Only Way I Want It*, named one of the Ten Best Books of 2009 by *The New York Times Book Review* and one of the best books of the year by *The Los Angeles Times* and Amazon.com. Her essays have appeared in *The New York Times*, *The Wall Street Journal*, and *The New Yorker*.

Kathleen Volk Miller's work has appeared in *Salon*, *The New York Times*, *Philadelphia* magazine, and several literary journals. She is coeditor of the anthology *Humor: A Reader for Writers* and the literary magazine the *Painted Bride Quarterly*; she also directs the graduate program in publishing and the Drexel Publishing Group at Drexel University. Currently she is working on a book, *Ramp Agent Parenting: Tales from a Grateful Mother*.

Lee Montgomery is a writer and editor living in Portland, Oregon.

Helen Oyeyemi was named one of *Granta*'s Best Young British Novelists in 2013. She is the author of five novels, including *Mr. Fox*, which won a 2012 Hurston/Wright Legacy Award, and *White Is for Witching*, which won a 2010 Somerset Maugham Award. Her most recent book is the story collection *What Is Not Yours Is Not Yours*.

Heather Sellers, who teaches at the University of South Florida, is the author of the memoir *You Don't Look Like Anyone I Know: A True Story of Family, Face Blindness, and Forgiveness*.

Lauren Slater is a psychologist and the author of a number of books, including *Opening Skinner's Box: Great Psychology Experiments of the Twentieth Century*, *Lying: A Metaphorical Memoir*, *Prozac Diary*, and *Welcome to My Country*. Her essays have appeared in *The New York Times*, *Harper's*, and *Elle*.

Susanna Sonnenberg has written two *New York Times* bestselling memoirs, *She Matters: A Life in Friendships* and *Her Last Death*, as well as a number of essays and reviews. She lives in Missoula, Montana.

Paige Williams is a staff writer at *The New Yorker*, an associate professor at the Missouri School of Journalism, and a former Nieman Fellow at Harvard. Her narrative nonfiction book, *The Dinosaur Artist*, is forthcoming from Hachette.